the
su

World record-winning gynaecological endoscopic surgeon Dr Rakesh
Sinha holds two Guinness World Records for his surgeries. The former
president of the Indian Association of Gynaecological Endoscopists,
he is a teacher, trainer, author and marathon runner. He is also
an internationally certified motivational speaker and a licentiate
practitioner for neuro linguistic Programming (NLP), and has been
featured on Jack Canfield's *Success Profiles.* Dr Sinha is the managing
director of Women's Hospital, a premier institute specializing in
minimal access surgery, and has also done a Post Doctorate Clinical
Fellowship in Endoscopy at the Royal Free Hospital in London. At
the time of going to press, he has thirty publications in international
index journals.

He is the proud parent of two doctors, and is a devoted son and
husband. He lives and works in Mumbai. This is his first book.

Dear Richard
Wishing you & yours
every success

Best wishes

Ratna Marker.
(my brother's legacy

Advance Praise for *The Anatomy of Success*

'Dr Rakesh Sinha has quite interestingly highlighted some of the essential virtues of success by sharing critical learnings drawn from his rich professional experience. I would agree that consistent efforts, a balanced mind, bold steps, openness to change and a clear conscience are intrinsic to success. Dr Sinha's disciplinary approach, positive disposition and quest for excellence are noteworthy qualities.'

– Deepak Parekh, chairman, HDFC

'I have personally known Dr Sinha for almost three decades and he is one of the best motivational speakers I have ever seen. His lecture sessions have really helped the Maharashtra Police. I would consider this book to be a masterpiece in the field of self development and management.'

– D. Sivanandhan, former commissioner of
Mumbai Police

'Two and a half minutes. 150 seconds. To make life-and-death decisions. From the gripping opening that starkly puts into perspective many of the decisions that business leaders agonize over – for days, weeks and sometimes months – as we strive to win, Dr Sinha's book meticulously unravels the science of being successful. Whether you are a student, early in your career or a seasoned executive, this book puts the steering wheel squarely in your own hands.'

– Kirthiga Reddy, managing director,
Facebook India

'*The Anatomy of Success* is a must read for anyone who aspires to be successful, whether they are a working professional, student, entrepreneur or a housewife. Elements like "thought is the starting point for action" and "choosing to choose" steer the reader towards success. Do not miss reading this work.'

– Jagdeep Kapoor, brand guru and author of
24 Brand Mantras

'Dr Sinha has brought his surgical precision to the success paradigm in a very readable book. I particularly liked his take on volition and willpower, both of which are key to successful decision-making.'

– Geeta Rao, former beauty health director,
Vogue India

'In *The Anatomy of Success*, Dr Sinha inspires, educates and equips us to firmly take control of our future and live up to our potential. This refreshing book draws on wisdom from Dr Sinha's experience and research in several diverse fields including medicine, motivational theory, general science, management, literature and neuroscience. You will find the book talking to your personal journey, with several insights distilled and communicated through powerful stories, experiences and practical tools. Whether you are a student, a young manager or an accomplished professional in search for further success, this thought-provoking book is well worth reading. More than once.'

– Vinay Hebbar, managing director, Asia Pacific,
Harvard Business Publishing

'*The Anatomy of Success* is a very deep read, and Rakesh has demonstrated that he is erudite and well-versed with medical terminology as well as motivational literature. In this book, he starts with the final destination of success and only *then* plans out the journey.

This book is a fantastic achievement, a true legacy. *The Anatomy of Success* is truly significant for a surgeon who has achieved much in a span of decades with extreme hard work, discipline, self-improvement and a major desire to succeed. Thank you for allowing me to read this. It has been an honour and a veritable pleasure.'

– Ratna Makker, consultant anaesthesiologist,
NHS, United Kingdom

'I recommend that this book not just be widely read by the masses but also in educational institutions where young minds are being shaped for the future.

Simple yet profound. I give it a five-star rating.'
— Dr Radhakrishnan Pillai, Department of Philosophy,
University of Mumbai
Author of *Corporate Chanakya, Chanakya's 7 Secrets of Leadership,
Chanakya in You*

'The theme of achieving success and culling the principles of success in the context of a life-and-death profession makes this book a gripping read. Above all, *The Anatomy of Success* convinces us that success is not the purview of a select few but that anyone who is serious enough to learn from Dr Sinha's experiences and has the courage to endure shall find success within his or her reach.'
— Pravin Kalawar, human potential consultant

'*The Anatomy of Success* is beautifully written and structured and is very different from a lot of the books on the subject.'
— Dr Abhijit Das, Senior Consultant, MD, International Institute of
Behavioral Studies, Sydney,
Senior Registrar
in Obstetrics/Gynaecology, Royal Hobart Hospital, Australia

'Dr Sinha's articulation of success through the metaphor of his practice is refreshing indeed. It also allows the reader to take a sneak peek at the complexities of the medical profession which could easily be extrapolated to challenges in different walks of life. Definitely a must-read for students of success.'
— Ninad Tipnis, Principal Architect, JTCPL Designs

'Excellent, fast-paced, well-researched and thorough.'
— Dr Harish Nadkarni, MD, healthcare quality consultant,
founder and director of Quality Care

'*The Anatomy of Success* is an entire treatise on the essential path to success, not on the structure of the human body, but on the anatomy of the mind, the psyche, the craving and passion for success, how it is generated, nurtured and reaches fruition. Dr Rakesh Sinha is a legendary teacher whose strength lies as much on 'Why' as 'How'. His language is simple, his message strong and he leaves an indelible impact on the open and eager mind.

This book needs study, digestion and absorption.'

– Dr Tehemton E. Udwadia, OBE, MS, FCPS,
FRCS (Eng.), FRCS (Ed.), FACS, FICS (Hon.),
FAMS, FARSI (Hon.)
Emeritus professor of surgery, Grant Medical College and J.J.
Hospital, consultant surgeon, Breach Candy Hospital, Parsee
General Hospital; chairman, Centre of Excellence for Minimal
Access Surgery Training (CeMAST)

'Meritocracy is all that should matter and mediocrity only leads to stunted growth. *The Anatomy of Success* undoubtedly is a MUST read as it is a flowing fountain of inspiration and hope. The messages that come through are concrete and clear.'

– Dr Sanjay Oak
Vice chancellor, DY Patil University, Mumbai

the anatomy of
success

MANAGEMENT LESSONS
FROM A SURGEON

DR RAKESH SINHA

with
Gayatri Pahlajani

Foreword by Jack Canfield

HarperCollins *Publishers* India

First published in India in 2016 by
HarperCollins *Publishers* India

P-ISBN: 978-93-5136-486-3
E-ISBN: 978-93-5136-487-0

2 4 6 8 10 9 7 5 3 1

HarperCollins *Publishers*
A-75, Sector 57, Noida, Uttar Pradesh 201301, India
1 London Bridge Street, London, SE1 9GF, United Kingdom
Hazelton Lanes, 55 Avenue Road, Suite 2900, Toronto, Ontario M5R 3L2
and 1995 Markham Road, Scarborough, Ontario M1B 5M8, Canada
25 Ryde Road, Pymble, Sydney, NSW 2073, Australia
195 Broadway, New York, NY 10007, USA

Typeset in 11/14.8 Adobe Garamond
by Saanvi Graphics Noida

Printed and bound at
Thomson Press (India) Ltd

To my parents, who gave me dreams

To my wife, Manju, who gave me unconditional love

To my children, Rinkita and Rushindra, who
gave me purpose

Contents

Part Three
THE COGNITIVE COMPONENT

Author's Note

Caesarean-section births are never the first port of call for any surgeon. Despite their popularity, delivering a baby surgically is usually the second of two options, the last of two resorts. From the time the mother is put under general anaesthesia and prepped for the birth, the surgeon just has a minuscule two-and-a-half-minute window from the skin incision to safely taking out the baby before it runs the risk of being compromised in the womb. A caesarean section, then, is as much an operation as it is a rescue operation.

Two and a half minutes. 150 seconds. That's nearly all the time any surgeon will ever have to safely bring a baby into this world.

It takes longer to make a cup of tea.

∽

For those of us working in the medical profession, the loudest sounds are usually the ones you cannot hear. The deafening silence that greets you when a formerly healthy thirty-eight-year-old person crashes on your operating table from a sudden cardiac arrest, or the disbelieving silence when you tell parents their daughter has just come out of a thirty-three-day coma. The loudest silences are usually heard when desperate hopes clash with the limitations of medical science or conversely, when medical science snatches life from the jaws of mortality. Every doctor, surgeon, nurse, technician or intern will probably experience at least one moment of silence that could have the power to either define them or destroy them. To those hearing it, it is the loudest sound in the world.

My moment of silence arrived in June 1986. Meera, a flight attendant with Air India, was wheeled into my operating theatre (OT) to deliver her first child. An earlier operation to remove fibroids from her uterus had left Meera with scar tissue all over her abdomen. And since you can't deliver a baby normally with that kind of scarring, it left me with no choice but to opt for a C-section.

When I walked into the OT, the patient was already under general anaesthesia and draped. I ran through my mental checklist: patient's vital signs, check; anaesthesia levels, check; baby's vital signs, check; instruments, check; diathermy, check. And – since I like to operate with music – Boney M, check.

'... *by the rivers of Babylon ...*'

I made the first cut, a six-inch incision on the skin over the abdomen, cutting through the first of five layers to reach the baby.

'*... where we sat down ...*'

The scalpel caught the light, glinting as I made my way through the next layer – subcutaneous fat. Two down, three to go.

'*... ye-eahhhh we wept ...*'

I cut through the rectal sheath, a protector of the muscle.

'*... when we remembered Zion ...*'

Muscle relented under the gentle persuasion of my knife, revealing the peritoneum, the innermost lining of the abdomen. I was nearly there.

'Forty-five seconds over, Rakesh,' said the attending paediatrician, keeping an eye on the clock. *So far so good*, I thought.

Like all surgeons doing a C-section in any OT in any part of the world, I was expecting the next incision to reveal the uterus. But when I made the cut, I was surprised by what I saw next.

Intestine.

Scar tissue from Meera's previous operation had penetrated far deeper than any test could reveal. It had formed over the uterus with the result that the neighbouring intestines had wound up sticking to the uterus. Like Velcro. Like a tree-hugging activist embracing the last tree on earth. The uterus was hidden by loops of intestine. I couldn't see the uterus. I had to deliver a baby in sixty seconds and *I couldn't see the uterus.*

My moment of silence had arrived.

Theoretically, it was no big deal. All I had to do was carefully separate the intestines (or bowel) from the uterus, cut open the uterus and deliver the baby. But this new complication needed time, and I didn't have time.

'Sixty seconds over, doctor,' said one of the nurses.

I didn't have a choice, either.

My hands worked deftly to separate the bowel from the uterus. I was a postgraduate teacher at the time and I tried to recall what I would tell my students. I could hear Professor Rakesh droning on in my head, 'Separate the bowel quickly, dissect the bladder peritoneum, push the bladder down, open the lower uterine segment, support the baby's head and deliver the baby.' But Surgeon Rakesh was screaming, *move, Move, MOVE!*

'120 seconds over, Dr Sinha.'

I had thirty seconds to go. Any longer than this and the baby could possibly drown in the amniotic fluid that was present in the womb. But I couldn't go any faster without damaging vital organs. If I rushed it, I could damage the intestine.

'150 seconds over, Rakesh!' The paediatrician's anxiety was escalating.

I had now exceeded the medically prescribed time limit for caesarean sections. Every second from now decreased the baby's chance of survival. My mind started to wander. I pictured coming out of the OT with a dead baby, telling Meera's husband, John, that we couldn't rescue his child because of complications caused due to 'dense bowel adhesions'. Would he even understand what that meant? I pictured Meera waking up from the anaesthesia, asking about her baby, but having no answer to give. I thought of the baby drowning in the womb.

I could feel the eyes of my entire surgical team on me. 'What's the matter, Rakesh?'

I don't think I can make it in time, I wanted to shout. The thought of the baby drowning in the womb.

'Three minutes, Rakesh! Please!' My paediatrician was in a panic.

I wanted to leave everything. I wanted to run home, crawl under a blanket and bury my head under a pillow. I wanted to disappear.

Finally, I made it. I reached the uterus and sliced through the membranes. A gush of amniotic fluid followed, after which I created a space large enough to pull the baby out. It was a boy.

I yanked his body out, holding his head and neck with my other hand. I wanted to look at his face and tell this newest entrant into the world, 'You gave us quite a scare.' And I probably would have, except that he was absolutely still.

He was limp.

His eyes were closed.

He wasn't breathing.

The silence in the operation theatre was deafening.

It was the loudest sound in the world.

The baby was motionless, not breathing.

That makes two of us, I thought.

I handed the baby over to the paediatrician. The OT suddenly burst into frenetic activity. All eyes on the baby. All hands on deck.

'Suction.'

'Catheter.'

'Warm towel.'

'Oxygen.'

'Keep the endotracheal tube ready.'

But I couldn't continue with the surgery. I just put in a surgical mop – a surgical sponge that absorbs blood and other fluids – and waited. I was looking at the paediatrician, at his face, for the final verdict. He looked up and nodded. And suddenly the baby cried.

That makes two of us, I thought.

'He's fine.'

'He's all right.'

'It's okay.'

Meera's 'baby' is now about thirty years old, healthy and active. He lives around my neighbourhood, but even after all these years it's never easy for me to see him or cross him in the street. Whenever I look at him, I still break out into a cold sweat. Because I know what he doesn't know – he almost didn't make it.

Meera's story taught me three things: failure is not an option, it isn't over until I win and, when I believe it, I can be unstoppable. I couldn't walk away from the table because that would have meant a dead baby. Her story also got me thinking – how different would people's lives be if they approach success the same way the medical profession does – *as if it were a matter of life and death*? In our jobs, in our daily lives, do we walk away too early? Do we genuinely do all we can do?

I don't think we do.

I don't think we do all we can do because we don't know what we can *really* do. Because we are, on some level, bound by the limits set for us, *by us*. And what a fallacy that is. Limits are self-imposed, man-made and a product of the way we think about ourselves. They reflect how confident – or under confident – we feel about our abilities, and in a sense, they are telling of whether we think we deserve the rewards they will bring. Quite simply, we're not born with limitations. We set them.

Most of us have, with a limited understanding of our potential, subconsciously created our own glass ceiling. But if we create, why can't we destroy? And with that, dive head first into a world of limitless possibility? That's why Meera's story – in addition to my commitment to my patients over the years – got me pushing other people into discovering their potential and helping them discover a world of unending possibilities on the other side of their hard-coded beliefs. I have trained doctors, the police and the CBI to maximize their own chances of being brilliantly successful using medical case studies, management theory and lessons learnt from surgical error. I have also drawn on different industries – like the airline industry – to motivate people to reduce errors and improve their results. And make them believe that they can do anything.

This book is a culmination of my work in surgery and motivational training. Welcome to *The Anatomy of Success*.

This is my story.

It could be yours.

Foreword

JACK CANFIELD

Nothing is as unforgiving as the medical profession – a split-second delay could translate into fatalities, a split-second distraction could translate into complications. But a split-second decision could save a leg, an arm, a spine, a heart or even bring someone back from the dead. While it is harsh and exhausting in equal measure, there is no greater glory than saving the life of a human being or improving the quality of life of countless others.

Whether they are aware of it or not, doctors, surgeons and nurses chase victory with desperate intent. They spend countless hours training and updating their skills. They take innumerable tests. They study for thousands of hours. Because of constant advances in medical research, they consistently fight to stay on top of their game, all with the intent of saving or improving the quality of a life. They know the fundamental rule about medicine: they either save a life or they don't; they either help alleviate suffering or they don't; black or white.

What can the medical profession teach us about success? What are the commonalities between management and medicine?

What can the medical profession teach us about beating the odds? About going beyond the brief? About being better than we ever could be?

When I interviewed Rakesh in Los Angeles for my DVD series *Success Profiles*, it was a real eye-opener. Here was this guy who was not only a successful, practising surgeon but a mine of information about motivational theory who taught me a thing or two. What I found even more remarkable was how deep he had gone into truly understanding what makes success successful.

Is being successful all about being lucky? Or brilliant? Is it the preserve of the genetically privileged? In this book, he argues that far from being the preserve of the genetically privileged, success is something we can wholeheartedly own because we are all *biologically privileged*. He expands our understanding of biological make-ups, the anatomical centres in the brain, neurophysiology, neurotransmitters, their effects on the body and our behaviour; how we as human beings can channel our biological gifts to achieve our dreams.

Rakesh also expounds on the fact that success can be taught, that successful habits can be acquired and he draws on inspiring real-life examples from both medicine and motivational theory to illustrate his point. He also wonders why everyone *doesn't* have a decidedly disciplined urge to succeed and focuses on understanding the demons chasing them. Can they be exorcised? He works with you on how to fight the most debilitating obstacle hampering your path to glory. Yourself.

Drawing from his surgical experiences – for which he holds two Guinness World Records – Doc motivates people to achieve excellence in their own professional goals by deconstructing success into simple, easy-to-grasp components, allowing you to see for yourself that success is something we are all deserving of. We all deserve to be successful. And we are what we believe.

Rakesh has been a student of anthropomaximology – the study of the higher potential of human beings – for about two decades. He has studied goal centredness, neuroanatomy, neurophysiology, neurobiology, cognitive psychology, psychoneuroimmunology and has graduated with a certification course in neurolinguistic programming (NLP). He has worked to qualify himself to write this book. And over and above all the lessons and theories and real-life experiences that this book will contain, Rakesh will continue to bring you back to the simple fact that no matter what you do or what your talents are, you need to chase victory with the same desperate intent as doctors do. Because, like medicine, a life does depend on whether you succeed or fail.

Yours.

Introduction
STUCK IN THE WAITING ROOM

Every year when the clocks turn over from 31 December to 1 January, you can almost hear the stroke of the midnight hour creak under the burden of countless unfulfilled and freshly-minted dreams. For so many, the new year represents hope and change. Or rather, the hope for change. Every year, as you wait for the clocks to turn over, you firmly make your resolution that *this* year will see you at the top of your career, *this* year will get you that corner office, *this* year you will make money like you never have before and *this* will be the year to achieve what you could only achieve in your dreams.

But as the months wear on and you stand at the cusp of yet another year, you wonder how January became November. You step back and take a look at yourself. You may have made incremental strides in your workplace, nudged your dreams in the right direction. Not the roaring success you were hoping for but you take comfort in the fact that you've done your best.

You're doing okay.

Are you okay with being okay? And have you *really* done your best?

Or are you simply waiting for the perfect moment, the perfect time, the perfect place to be as successful as you want to be? Are you waiting for things to come to you but increasingly getting the feeling that you are continually in transit, never truly reaching your final destination? Are you *stuck* in the waiting room?

What are you waiting for, exactly?

Waiting is not necessarily a bad thing. Good surgeons wait for the right time to operate. To paraphrase Dr Paul Ruggieri in his book *Confessions of a Surgeon*, the first ten years of medical practice are spent learning *how* to operate, the next ten are spent learning *when* to operate and the next ten are spent learning when *not* to operate. But the decision to wait is only made when anomalies have been ruled out, tests have been conducted, suspicious growths identified, blood workups done and full investigations carried out. When it comes to surgical intervention, waiting is always the last box to tick off, if at all.

If you aren't reaching where you want to be, have you diagnosed the problem and set a treatment course for yourself? Have you really changed the way you approach your professional life? Have you really revolutionized the way you work? Or are you doing the same thing over and over again, waiting patiently for glory because waiting is the *only* strategy you have employed? Hope, by itself with no correctives in place, is not a good success strategy. We will start your journey into transforming your professional life with the conviction that you *can* change. But whether you believe you can, though, depends significantly on how you talk. To yourself.

What's Your Label?

We're label mongers. From the time we are in kindergarten our teachers, friends, parents and even strangers have their own labels for us, and we do for them. To your parents, you may be the obedient child. To your children, you may be the lenient parent. To your colleagues, you may be the one that likes to copy everyone on all emails. To your hairdresser, you may be the big tipper.

But it's the damaging labels that others put on us or we put on ourselves that hinder our path to growth: 'lazy', 'fat', 'loser', 'average'. Once these labels start to chip away at our self-esteem, we start to believe them ourselves. We start living up to the potential of our limited beliefs, good or bad. We become boxed in by our perceived limitations instead of surpassing them. Say you are not who you are now. Let's say you are the only child of not one, but two extremely accomplished surgeons. You have grown up in the company of brilliance. But try as you may, you may not be able to match their genius. Your skills may lie in other directions: maybe you're artistic or good with words. But because your innate talents are different from your parents', you may always feel that you will be in the shadow of two people you have tried to impress your whole life. What would you call yourself then? What will be the label you choose for yourself? Do these labels inspire you or do they keep you where you've always been? *Stuck* in the waiting room?

End the wait. It doesn't matter what people around you think or even what you think of yourself; you can achieve independently of your labels. If people around you don't think you can become a doctor, actor, writer or singer, that is entirely their opinion. What they say to you doesn't matter. It's what you say to *yourself* that matters most. Change your labels. Change your life. What others think of you is none of your business.

You can achieve independently of your limitations. Whether you're short or tall, flush with funds or completely broke, it shouldn't matter. As the child of a school teacher and a social worker, I wanted to go to Germany to train in endoscopy but I couldn't afford it. But I just *had* to. The belief that the training programme could alter the course of my entire career, and therefore my professional and financial future, only propelled me to see *solutions*, not obstacles. After many days of chewing on the problem, I realized I had one asset that I could sell. And I was sitting on it! I went to Germany by selling off my motorbike. It wasn't an easy decision to make. It was a gorgeous Royal Enfield Bullet. It was my life, my pride, my joy. Selling it was something I struggled with greatly. But it was, till date, one of the best decisions I have ever made.

As Joe Dispenza says, you can achieve independently of your environment. You can thrive despite your environment, despite the family you live with or the background you come from. It's *how* you emerge from your environment that dictates the course of your future. The former president of India – A.P.J. Abdul Kalam – was the son of a boat maker who could barely afford his school fees. He could have dreamt a dream more 'suited' to his background. But he chose to father India's nuclear programme. He achieved, he shone, he conquered. Independent of his environment.

You can achieve independently of your past. The past belongs firmly in the past. What you did before, whether it worked or not doesn't matter. Your tomorrow depends on your today. To quote Jim Rohn, 'You must make tomorrow an important part of your current philosophy,' or Les Brown, 'It doesn't matter where you come from. The only thing that matters is where you are heading.' Today is the cleanest, freshest start you will ever have: a *tabula rasa,* as it were – a clean slate. Let go of your past professional mistakes. Become all you can become.

You can achieve independently of your genes, as Joe Dispenza says. Everybody is born with different genes – maybe some more predisposed towards achieving success and wealth – but anatomically, everyone inherits similar brain structures. There are centres for decision-making, there are neurotransmitters and neurochemicals, there are neural pathways that dictate our actions. All of these can be used to chart a new course that can lead you to victory independent of the genes you were born with. Which is what we will talk about in greater detail in the chapter 'The Science of Change'.

But why write this book? What's in it for me? I'm a full-time surgeon and all I know is that nothing unsettles me more than watching people *not* live up to their potential. When I see someone down-and-out, fatalistic, despondent, seeing no hope for the future or belief in their abilities, it makes me want to shake them out of their self-imposed stupor. Because it's all there; your potential is lying dormant, waiting to be discovered.

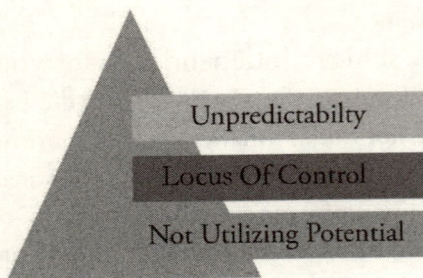

The Three Stressors

Not utilizing your potential, psychologists say, is a huge stressor. Which is why almost every motivational speaker, international trainer or anyone else in this field is looking to tap untapped potential to include Jack Canfield in his Human Potential Movement. As Benjamin Franklin once said, 'We are all sundials in the shade.' We all have tremendous potential, but it is undiscovered, hidden and shy, like a sundial deprived of the thing it needs the most. Is it possible then for you to *allow* your talents to see the light?

One of the things we have in common with the most successful people in the world – be it presidents, CEOs, state leaders, celebrities, star athletes – is that they all have 1440 minutes in a day, 5,25,600 minutes in a year, just like us. It is how we utilize every minute that decides how successful we are going to become. How do you see the rest of the minutes you have left on the clock? What do you want to do with them?

This is not to recognize that genuine problems like an ailing spouse or parent or a depressed market in recession don't exist, and can hamper or set your goals back. But working towards ensuring your own professional future is about assuring yourself that waiting is the *last* strategy you have employed, and not the first. You're not *stuck* where you are. You're there because you want to be, voluntarily. If you are indeed waiting, you are simply waiting for the changes you have made to pay off.

If you look at success under a microscope, you will find that it's not one big, amorphous blob but is actually composed of three very distinct components. *The Anatomy of Success* is, therefore, a book in three parts because I believe that success, like motivation, is made is made up of three parts:

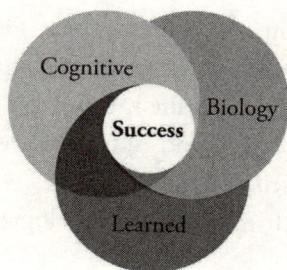

The Three Components of Success

Biology – or what you're born with.
Learning – your environment or what you learn along the way.

Cognitive – or how you think and how driven you are to achieve success.

While we know we are biologically predisposed to succeed and build successful habits – which I will elaborate in 'The Science of Change' – what we learn and how motivated we are to achieve success is also crucial to our victory parade. Any raw biological predisposition is meaningless if not harnessed by learning the right lessons. And learning, in turn, is meaningless if you don't have that will, that inner urge, that *desperation* to make something of your life.

To that end, the first component, i.e., **Biology**, will talk about how your brain works and what can be done with it to enhance your chances of success. The second component, i.e., **Learning**, will detail what you can learn from medical examples and will also include other lessons learnt from a life-and-death profession so that you can 'learn' success. The third and final component, i.e., **Cognition,** emphasizes that you can't achieve success in any sphere of your life if you don't have the thought process and the will to get ahead and elaborates on what you can do to motivate yourself.

We first start with part one, the biological component to success.

One of the things I like about medicine the most is that it's a great leveller. We are all born with similar physiologies: one brain, two kidneys, two lungs and one big heart. Our brain has been in development for six million years, which means that we have survived and *thrived* where other species have become extinct, forever consigned to the depths of history. By virtue of that, as humans, the last six million years have shown us that we are all *biologically* predisposed to succeed. And with that knowledge we can discard the past, free of the labels we impose on ourselves. We can use our biology to change our current reality and shape our tomorrows irrespective of our yesterdays.

That's why biology is so liberating. That's why biology is freedom.

Part One

THE BIOLOGICAL COMPONENT

CHAPTER ONE

The Science of Change

You're in a cardiologist's office. You are nervous. You've barely slept the night before. You have been breathless for the last two weeks and your GP suspects heart disease. He has referred you to the heart specialist in whose waiting room you are now sitting. You spend a disproportionate amount of time staring at his degrees mounted on the wall. Anything to distract yourself. By the time you are called in, you know his qualifications better than you know yours.

Your ECG indicates arrhythmia, i.e., irregular heartbeat and some changes. This, coupled with the symptoms you are exhibiting, could possibly mean coronary heart disease, the specialist says while recommending additional tests. You're a thirty-eight-year-old man. You were not expecting this.

You don't remember how you got home. But the next thing you remember is googling 'Coronary Heart Disease' and reading, 'Coronary heart disease (CHD) is the leading cause of death … worldwide.'[1]

Death. Another sleepless night.

By the time you wake up the next morning – can you still call it waking up if you haven't slept? – there is a dull pain in your left arm that you haven't previously felt and a tightness in your chest, suspiciously similar to the symptoms you read about the night before. New day, new symptoms. You start to wonder if this is the beginning of the end. You start thinking of how you need to legalize, notarize, formalize your affairs for your wife/ child/mother/brother/dog.

The phone rings. It's the cardiologist's office. Could you come down to the office for a second on your way to work? Of course, you say, but with an even tighter chest. On your drive there, you feel overwhelmed by breathlessness. Will you pass out behind the wheel?

The staff at the cardiologist's clinic do a re-test. It was a false alarm. Your ECG was normal all along. A mix-up of your papers with another patient's. The clinic is profusely apologetic. The cardiologist now thinks you're probably anaemic after hearing

---

1   http://www.nhs.uk/Conditions/Coronary-heart-disease/Pages/ Introduction.aspx; Last Accessed on 11 May 2016

about your diet; anaemia, probably caused by iron deficiency. Nothing to worry about. As suddenly as it came, the tightness in your chest vanishes. The shortness of breath has reduced to a gentle murmur. No big clouds looming over the horizon. The forecast promises sound sleep.

Psychoneuroimmunology (PNI) is the study of the link between your mind and your health. 'For more than a decade, researchers have known that behavioural and psychological events can influence the immune system.'[2] The tightness in your chest, the significant shortness of breath was in most part brought on by the *fear* of a condition that you still hadn't been diagnosed with. That the brain can manipulate you *physiologically* is indicative of how beautifully **powerful** it is. The question then is, can you use its powers for good?

The human brain is the centre for everything we do – how we think, act and feel. And the way we think is the reality we create for ourselves; a reality that also determines whether we succeed or we fail. No matter who we are or where we come from, we all have about the same composition of brains. It is composed of 78 per cent water, 10 per cent fat, 8 per cent protein with other assorted components that cover the final 4 per cent. But even at that small size, it still consumes about a fifth or 20 per cent of the oxygen intake, about a third of our body's water and a massive 40 per cent of the nutrients extracted from the blood. We also have 100 *billion* neurons and 1 million *miles* of nerve fibres. Your brain is quite literally the

---

2 http://www.apa.org/monitor/dec01/anewtake.aspx; Last Accessed on 11 May 2016

nerve centre for decisions; decisions that decide whether you win or lose, succeed or fail.

Success, quite literally, is all in your head.

But if that's what lumps us together, why are we so different? Why do some of us stand at the periphery of success, watching others sweep in and take the prize? Why is someone else's grass *actually* greener? I'll start at the beginning or, in other words, what we are born with.

Genes.

There's a gene for just about anything and everything we have. We have genes for height, for hair, genes that will determine whether we age early or later. We have genes for whether we can make jokes or whether we can take them. We also have genes for intelligence – the long arm of chromosome 6 IGF2R – as well as genes for our personality, which is dictated by the short arm of chromosome 11 D4DR, also called the personality gene. 'She was born to swim' is what you would probably say for someone who has an inherent talent for taking to the water. 'He has a nose for business,' is what you may say for someone who looks like they emerged from the womb with a current account and a calculator. Studies show that many aspects of our lives – right from whether we are focused or distracted to whether we have great amounts of self-control to whether we are persistent – boil down to our genetic inheritance. What we like or hate, whether we're sporty or have feet that itch to travel, all these are genetically determined. If you're reading this right now, trying hard to fight your past and looking to the future while blaming your genes, this doesn't look good right now, does it?

Let me also bring in some research. In the year 2000, the Cold Spring Harbour Laboratory Genome Meeting started a cheeky little game called GeneSweep: since the number of genes we are born with is *still* unknown, the participants started an informal betting pool to estimate how many genes we have inherited. The winning bet – because it was in line with the existing gene-prediction programmes – was put in by Lee Rowen of the Institute of Systems Biology in Seattle. The winning number? 25,947.

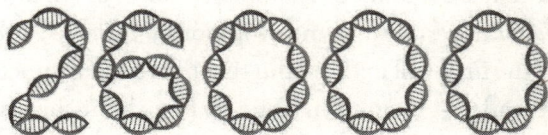

Yikes. About 26,000 genes. Or in other words, about 26,000 determinants that either pull you towards or take you away from that CEO trajectory. Or about 26,000 new ways to blame your current situation on. Or about 26,000 brand new excuses to explain why you are where you are. It seems all tied up in a neat little bow. You want to throw in the towel? You want to give up? Don't.

To some extent, yes, you *are* born with a predisposition to success. You are not wrong. But you *are* wrong to think that your gene pool spells the end and not the beginning of your final goal. Genes also sometimes work in tandem with the environment. They don't, for example, make you prone to bungee jumping at inopportune moments, but they do ensure that if you would like to leap off a bridge with nothing more to save you from a violent death than a giant rubber band, you will thoroughly enjoy the experience. This also means that many of your genes are *dormant,* waiting to emerge on the other side of that rubber band. In other words, unless you take the leap, *how do you know whether you will like it or not?* With approximately 26,000 estimated indicators to predisposition, can you safely say that you have discovered *every* single like, dislike or tendency? Are you *so* sure that you don't have it in you to succeed? Even if you *think* you've really tried? I'm willing to bet – since I suspect I have a betting gene – that you haven't.

Our brain is the result of six million years of development and it has *doubled* in size since the evolution of humans. It has also survived the final nail in the coffin that put so many other species six-foot-under – extinction. The human brain has survived millions of years of drought, famine, extreme cold and extreme heat by finding the best way to live. From not knowing how to light a fire, it has discovered medical miracles, cars, cell phones and space travel. Even if you dig deep, into the deepest part of yourself that no one knows exists but you, and you still feel like you haven't succeeded at being successful, please remember that despite what we are born with or *think* we are born with, the human brain – by virtue of being the *human* brain – is designed for success and for us to achieve mastery over anything we want. And we have six million years of survival to show for it.

Now for the research I think you will like. Scientists have learnt more about the brain in the past decade than they have in the last 5,000 years[3] and what they've learnt is that while genes do influence our behaviour (and therefore, our ability to develop successful habits) they do *not* account for all of what we do. **Our**

---

3   *The Brain DVD*, New York: History, 2008

final behaviour – and therefore success – is shaped by not one, not two, but *three* components:

1. What we are born with. Or **Biology**, which includes inherited genes but also brain components, neurotransmitters and other chemical messengers common to *all* humans.

2. What new information we have picked up along the way. Or **Learning**.

3. How we think about success and whether we *want* – or have the inner urge – to do well. Or **Cognition**.

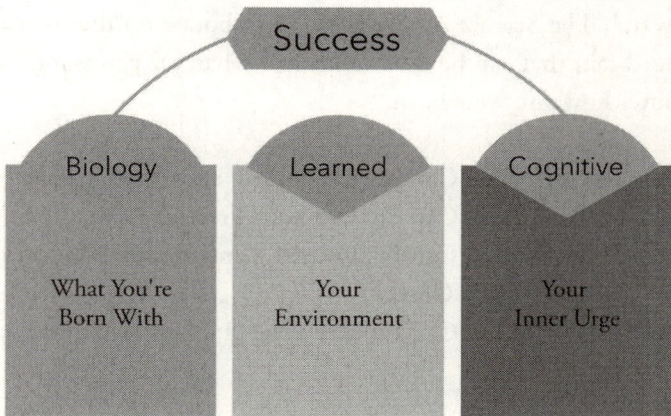

Learning and volition combine with biological predisposition to make us who we are. It is no longer nature *versus* nurture. *It is nature and nurture that determine the final outcome.* Put that in your pipe and smoke it; if developing addictive habits – and therefore smoking – is in your genes.

But that's not how we started this chapter, if you remember. At the start, I essentially established the idea that success is all in your head. And it is. Despite our genes, there are parts of the brain which can be realigned, their functions manipulated and steered on course to get to where we want to be. If we really *want* to, that is. The brain is not set in stone. It is quite the opposite, in fact. Think of the brain as a toolkit, a delightfully delectable buffet of options that would make or break our entire future. Despite what we were born with.

Instead of looking at what genes you *don't* have compared to the world's most successful people, have you ever looked at what you *do* have in common with them? 'The Science of Change' will elaborate on the parts of your brain that can be used to achieve whatever you want. No matter how you were born.

1. To Be All You Can Be, Use Your **Neurotransmitters.**
2. To Be All You Can Be, Use Your **Frontal Lobe.**
3. To Be All You Can Be, Use the **Ventromedial Aspect of the Prefrontal Cortex.**
4. To Be All You Can Be, Use Your **Nucleus Accumbens.**

Neurotransmitters

The Journey of a Thought

Everything we do, whether it is instinctively looking for traffic before crossing the road, brushing our teeth or the unique way we eat noodles, is composed of a series of nerve cells that send information to each other. Without exception, we first *think* before we do. For example, the simple act of brushing your teeth starts off as a thought. Nerve cells – also called neurons – located in your brain transmit the message to the neurons in your spinal cord, which in turn pass the message on to your hand to pick up that toothbrush. While all this happens in a matter of *milliseconds*, it is this series of neural conversations – also called a neural circuit – that translates thought into action.

Hebb's Law states that 'nerve cells that fire together, wire together.' In other words, if you repeatedly stimulate the same nerve cells, they will keep leading to the same actions where it will start becoming a part of your involuntary or habitual behaviour. And the longer you maintain a particular habit or think in a particular way, the more your brain becomes hardwired to *retain* that habit or mindset. In other words, you become neurochemically bound to your existing, familiar life.

Neurotransmitters are described as 'chemical messengers' that transmit signals between these nerve cells, enabling communication between the brain and the nervous system. In other words, between thought and action. Neurotransmitters can transmit any *message you want*. An inspiring one, a positive one or one drenched in defeat.

You want something? *Think* it first. Your thoughts are all in *your* control, all in your hands. Or rather, all in your head. The question is, what thoughts do you want to send?

The Frontal Lobe

THE PART OF THE BRAIN THAT RESPONDS TO CHANGE

Known as the CEO of the brain, the frontal lobe is that part of the brain which separates us from the rest of the animals. Among

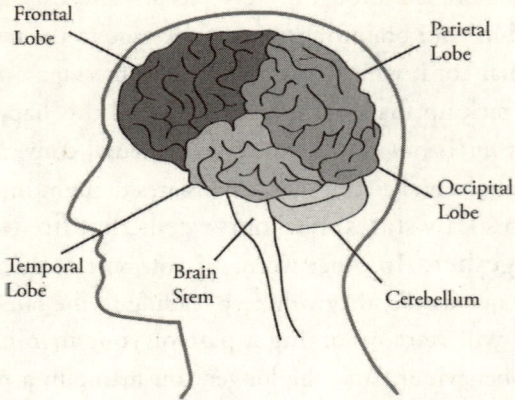

Your Brain

the key functions that it performs, the frontal lobe dictates the choices we make and is also the seat of discipline, planning, impulse control and free will. It is the control room of the 'self', which is a human being's greatest expression. It controls how the rest of the brain operates and oversees *all* brain activities. It also directs your focus and this becomes particularly important when you are overloaded with information. The human brain, scientists have estimated, can store ten *trillion* bits of memory and – are you sitting down for this? – processes 400 *billion* bits of data every *second*. But thanks to the frontal lobe, it narrows it down to only 2,000 bits and in this brilliant downsizing activity, it enables us to concentrate on specific things. Significantly, the frontal lobe is also that part of the brain which both creates and responds to change. It is what allows you to change course.

But are we using our frontal lobe to its full potential? Phineas Gage, an American railroad worker in the mid-1800s, was seriously injured in a routine explosion to create a passageway for railway tracks.

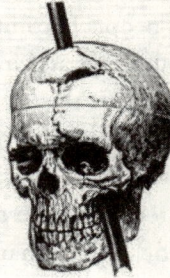

Phineas Gage   Illustration of the Rod Piercing his Skull

In the accident, an iron rod pierced his head right through his left frontal lobe. While he miraculously survived and went on to live a normal life, his friends remarked that he was no longer himself. The damage to his frontal lobe had brought out such significant personality changes in him that from being regarded as a model employee, he became verbally abusive and found it hard to stick to a schedule or follow a plan. His employers, a construction company, were subsequently unwilling to take him back.[4] Known as 'Neuroscience's Most Famous Patient',[5] Phineas Gage was one of the earliest known cases that suggested a connection between personality changes and brain injury.

---

4   http://www.smithsonianmag.com/history/phineas-gage-
    neurosciences-most-famous-patient-11390067/?no-ist; Last
    Accessed on 11 May 2016
5   Ibid

About a century ago, the surgical extraction of the frontal lobe of the brain – in a procedure known as a lobotomy – was also the chosen 'corrective' treatment for criminals, highly aggressive patients and prisoners. Surgical removal of the frontal lobe resulted in people becoming lethargic, lazy and disinterested in their surroundings and in their life.

The removal of this part of the brain was also deeply associated with compulsive routine behaviour like wearing the same clothes every day, eating at the same time every day and it could even include listening to the same things every day, like the radio. Introduction of any change to this set routine could result in the emotional breakdown of these individuals. *Change was, therefore, the enemy.* The same actions were performed with the same results and that is how their lives were lived. Day in and day out. The same.

Does this sound familiar? Do we live like this? With a huge fear of change, with the inability to progress, doing the same things every day, working the same way, making the same mistakes? Are we going through life without really stimulating this major part of our brain? Are we living like we do *not* have a frontal lobe?

If we learn how to use our frontal lobe, we possess the ability to create our future. We possess the ability to control the development of our careers. We possess the ability to control how much money we make. What we need to do is manipulate the workings of this section of our brain to our advantage. We can do this by doing new things – by changing the way we work and, to paraphrase Joe Dispenza, breaking the habit of being ourselves.

The best part about the frontal lobe of the brain is that it is unhindered by genes and can be changed by volition and learning. One of the best ways to stimulate it is by engaging in novel experiences whether it means reading something new, watching a new movie, going out with new friends or going to a new restaurant or country. Or in terms of professional growth, taking on a new challenge, a training course or even something small like changing the order in which you answer your emails. Anything new that you do stimulates your frontal lobe. People who fall into a rut go to the same place of work, take the same route, follow the same exercise pattern, have the same friends, visit the same places. It then becomes hard to change the existing state of mind. So many bestsellers are written in cafes for example; they represent a different environment and stimulate the brain. Doing new things is the starting point of stimulating neurons to create new neural pathways.

Another way to stimulate your frontal lobe and to change the way you think is to ask **open-ended** questions like 'What if?'[6] The moment you ask yourself, 'What if I were to write a book?' or 'What if I were to start my own business?' or 'What if I changed my way of working?', it challenges your existing line of thought, stimulates your frontal lobe and suddenly introduces you to a whole new set of approaches. Do a simple exercise. Say you'd like to bump up your earnings. Instead of telling yourself *I need to make more money,* ask yourself, *How can I make more money?* Which of the two approaches works better? Which is more inspiring? And which generates more solutions? See for yourself.

---

6 Joe Dispenza, *Evolve Your Brain: The Science of Changing Your Mind*, India: Westland, 2008

Open-ended questions enable us to better understand what we want and how we want to change. This enables us to be the architects of our future as it is the starting point for behavioural modifications. Isn't it amazing? By simply changing your approach to problem solving from a *close-ended to an open-ended approach*, you've opened your mind to endless possibilities. And with that, opened a door to a new you.

BE THE CHANGE YOU WANT TO BE

Want to get a jumpstart on making changes in your life? Stimulate your frontal lobe by asking open-ended questions like:

- HOW can I get new projects?
- HOW can I publicize my project?
- HOW can I get new clients?
- HOW can I get to the next level at work?
- HOW can I contribute to this project?
- HOW can I get my boss to notice my work?
- HOW can I get an overseas posting?
- What can I do differently?
- HOW can I earn more?
- HOW can I afford a new house?
- HOW can I buy a new office?
- What if I could do this differently?

The Ventromedial Aspect of the Prefrontal Cortex

CHANGE THE WAY YOU MAKE DECISIONS

Right from brushing your teeth in the morning to refusing a cigarette to deciding how to reply to a text message or email, you make decisions pretty much every waking hour of every day. Noted academic Sheena Iyengar, in her book *The Art of Choosing,*[7] has further estimated that humans make thirty-five decisions *every day* that affect their professional lives.[8] Which, in other words, translates into thirty-five possibilities every day to forge ahead in your career or thirty-five ways to set you back. In some cases, the decisions you take at your workplace can have an even wider implication. Say you have a company with 100 employees and each of them make thirty-five professional decisions a day. As the head of the company, you will then have 3,500 decisions taken daily that affect your business.

Decision-making, simply put, has exponential implications.

When you make decisions, you employ the ventromedial aspect of the prefrontal cortex. It is that part of the frontal lobe which has your decision-making centre and is the seat for the decisions you make, good or bad. While we will get into greater detail about decision-making centres in the ensuing pages, all you have to note for now is that the more options the brain has, the more difficult is the choice and so the fewer options given to the brain, the better the decision-making ability. This phenomenon is called the Paradox of Choice, and is a term attributed to Barry Schwartz.

---

7   Sheena Iyengar, *The Art of Choosing*, London: Abacus, 2011
8   Ibid

I find myself doing this with my patients now. I remember a time I used to sit with them and present six options for treatment. By the time I came to the sixth one, the patient used to frown and say something along the lines of, 'I can't decide, Dr Sinha. I'll tell you tomorrow.' Because by now I had confused her entirely.

I now find myself shortlisting the best possible options and trying to present the patient with no more than *two* options, which I discovered helps them make up their minds. Don't give too many choices to anyone, even yourself. If you find five ways to get that corner office, whether it's assigning yourself more responsibility so that you have more professional visibility or delegating more to your juniors, narrow down the options that you should follow. Too many options lead to procrastination. While we will explore the art and science of decision-making later in this book in a separate chapter, 'Choosing to Choose: Understanding Decision-Making', what's important for you to know now is that if you want to change your reality and therefore your future, change the way you make decisions.

The Nucleus Accumbens
THE PART OF THE BRAIN THAT RESPONDS TO CHALLENGES

Located within the dorsal striatum of your brain, the Nucleus Accumbens (NA) is that part of you which is chiefly responsible for responding to a challenge and gives you the 'revved up' feeling when you're confronted with something oppositional. When faced with a challenge, this part of the brain fuels you with determination and motivation, spurring you into action. However, for the NA to be activated, the challenge has to be significant to you.

As described by Daniel Pink in his book *Drive,* when your NA is being challenged, it taps into your emotional experiential memory – located in the deeper part of your amygdala – and together both work to give you a neurological 'push' that kicks you out of your comfort zone. What this tells us is that contradiction and friction are good. If you're being criticized, get inspired. If you're being left out, claw your way back in. The more opposition you have in your life, the more responsive the NA gets, the more chances you get to become constructive and, consequently, productive. Maybe that's why so many success stories feature people who have lived the early parts of their lives in poverty or adversity. They were being challenged all the time.

In order to stimulate your NA, the next time you are being opposed, tell yourself the challenge is important to you. Doing so sends a message to your NA which will work together with your amygdala and help spark a response. It will lead you to a solution that's not just better, but deeper.[9]

The Anatomy of the Rut

But all this sounds good, you say. So then why do we stay the same?

Well, for most part, we are who we *think* we are and if we think in the same way repeatedly, our realities are repeated. And if we repeatedly live the same reality, we will live the same lives. But before we understand how to change our life to attain glorious success, it is important to first understand how and why we stay the same. To first understand the anatomy of the **rut**.

---

9   Daniel H. Pink, *Drive: The Surprising Truth About What Motivates Us*, Edinburgh: Canongate, 2009

Is There Such a Thing as an Evil Brain?

While morality – and the concept of right and wrong – is in our genes, why are some brains good and some 'evil'? Scientists studying the brains of psychopaths have learnt that they have smaller amygdalas – at an average 18 per cent smaller volume than normal[10] – reducing their capacity for empathy and compassion and setting their moral compass haywire. In these cases, scientists believe that the amygdala and the frontal lobe do not talk to each other. The implication of this is that as the frontal lobe is the seat of control over impulses and emotions, it could make the difference between controlling impulses and acting on them. White-collar criminals, on the other hand, do have smaller amygdalas than normal but unlike psychopaths, their amygdalas seem to communicate with their frontal lobes correctly and while they have a reduced capacity for empathy, they are more prone to lying and cheating as opposed to homicidal, murderous or more advanced criminal behaviour.

How and what we think is also dictated by the environment we are a part of. Where we live, the people that surround us, what we are told about ourselves, the conditions that we survive under, they all contribute to a particular – and familiar – way of thinking, living and doing. It is said that *you are the product of the five people you meet the most every day.* They could be your

10 http://www.livescience.com/13083-criminals-brain-neuroscience-ethics.html; Last Accessed on 18 May 2016

parents, your friends, your colleagues, your co-workers. Familiar places, people, routines and environments trigger the same neural pathways, galvanize the same network of nerve cells which trigger familiar thoughts which lead to familiar, repetitive actions. And repetitive actions lead to the same results.

A rut is therefore nothing but a series of comfortable, familiar habits owing to neurons that follow the same path every second of every day to give you the desired result. These could be any sort of habits – social, hygiene, relationship and even work habits. The consistent achievement of excellence is a habit. But then, so is mediocrity. It depends on what we have taught ourselves to do over and over again. This is probably why we stay the same.

Ah, but if that's where it could end, it would. Ladies and gentlemen, let me tell you that even as you're reading this, absorbing the words and wondering what comes next, there is a war going on in your head: the ultimate push-and-pull, give-and-take, left-or-right kind of tug-of-war. It is the ultimate battle between the old and the new. Tapping your frontal lobe, nucleus accumbens and the rest can lead to a whole new you, but there is a constant fight in your brain between the parts that want change and the part that wants you to stay the same, which is the amygdala. This part of the brain craves routine and the repetition of habits. It desperately wants you to revert to the familiar. This part revels in the sameness and tries to ensure that you avoid returning to the unknown. It is *also* why we struggle to change.

There is an evolutionary reason for this. In the days when people were hunter-gatherers and not much else, the amygdala prevented them from entering unknown territory or plunging into certain death. Routine and familiarity were not just matters of comfort, but a matter of *survival:* it kept them alive and prevented them from venturing into the unknown. But venturing into the unknown is precisely what the nature of change is and to that end, when you are trying to change your age-old habits this evolutionary response is what you need to fight. The older the habit, the harder the fight.

The amygdala is also the seat of emotions, which could explain why you sometimes make decisions based on emotions. Since the decision-making centre is located in the frontal lobe, the frontal lobe and the amygdala 'talk' to each other when you're making a decision. I'll explain what I mean: you're driving home after a long, tiring, stressful day and there is bumper-to-bumper traffic as far as the eye can see. But suddenly things change and the road opens up. You eagerly grab your chance and speed up a little. Just as you're getting into the groove, a cab driver zooms past and tries to cut you off, nearly clipping your bumper in the process. Both of you brake hard in the middle of the road and before you even realize it, you are out of the car and are grabbing the cab driver's collar, holding up equally angry commuters behind you. It's all blaring horns and blood rushing to your head.

Road rage is a primary example of what happens when the frontal lobe 'loses' and the amygdala takes over; when emotion wins over self-control. Rage is a negative emotional response and the decisions you take when you're enraged sometimes have consequences which stay long after that near-accident, that big fight or when that drama is over. While the frontal lobe usually controls the amygdala, there are times when it loses the battle.

And it's not just rage. Sometimes, more positive emotions also 'win', leaving you unable to make bigger changes in your life to include emotions like loyalty, familiarity and comfort. This could be why you've been doing the same job for years or the reason you're stuck in a bad marriage. It is not just the amygdala's function as a habit centre, but its function as the seat of emotions could also be what is keeping you in the rut.

Breaking the Rut

IT ALL STARTS WITH THINKING THAT YOU CAN.

You are a mid-level executive and your annual review is coming up in three months. Your boss drops big fat glorious hints that you may not get promoted. Based on your past performance – the consistent, set pattern of your work habits – he doesn't think you have what it takes. You don't care what he thinks. What is unchanged is your desire to get that corner office. What you need to change are your work habits. What should you do?

In his book *Breaking the Habit of Being Yourself*, Dr Joe Dispenza says, 'Just by changing our thoughts, feelings, emotional reactions and behaviour, we send our cells new signals, and they express new proteins without changing the genetic blueprint.'[11] If you want to lose thirty kilos, win a gold medal, climb Mount Everest, you cannot do it in the comforting lap of familiarity. According to neuroscientists, your brain – and therefore your behaviour – can be transformed by just thinking differently because without exception, thought is the starting point for action.

---

11 Joe Dispenza, *Breaking the Habit of Being Yourself: How to Lose Your Mind and Create a New One*, Carlsbad, California: Hay House, 2012

We can't expect our lives to change if we think the same, act the same and experience the same every day. To change work habits, to get that promotion, to reach the highest level, you need to do something you have not done in the past. Success is not out of your league. It is simply out of your comfort zone. And getting out of your comfort zone starts off with changing the way you think.

But is it really that simple? How do you change the way you think? Well, you just do. You take a target, a dream, a thought, an old regret or a new ambition and let it set up camp in your mind. You picture your brain as a giant camping ground with endless acres of space, just waiting for your dreams to pitch their tents. You drive your dreams into this ground with stakes and tie them tightly so they hang on, even when life takes over. That's the beautiful thing about thoughts. They don't cost money. They don't see limits unless *you have* imposed them. The longer you give them life, the longer they live. And the longer they live, the longer they persist despite the noise in your mind, increasing your chances of following through with them. The best part is that the brain *likes* to take risks, in that humans by nature seek risks. If we didn't, we wouldn't be living in cities. We'd still be living in caves.

But why do dreams die? I believe that there is both a simple answer and a complex one. The simple answer is that dreams die because you let them. As the sole custodian of your ambition, the longevity of your dreams depend on how fragile your ability is to hold on to them. This in turn could depend on whether they are being subjected to environments that are hostile to their nurturing. Are your dreams vulnerable to your inner environment, i.e., do your negative thoughts have more power than your positive thoughts? Are your dreams vulnerable to your outer environment? Do the people or situations around you discourage you from hanging on to them?

The more complex answer, I think, is that dreams die because you may not believe they are important enough to hang on to in the first place. Your family, your spouse, your financial commitments or health could alter the path of many ambitions you set out to achieve and it is a choice that you have made. Or sometimes, dreams change, ambitions change. What you thought you wanted may not be what you wanted at all. A potential CEO may suddenly want to change tack and take up organic farming; a stockbroker may want to give it all up and backpack around the world on a shoestring budget. Sometimes, one ambition clashes with another and then it becomes about prioritizing which ambition is more important. But if you've let your dream go, you should feel that you have let it go in peace; that it hasn't been wrenched from you. You have voluntarily and happily let go; upon reflection, it was not a dream *meant* for you.

This part, and in fact this book, seeks to work with those who have let their dreams go simply because they didn't *believe* that they could be where they wanted to be; they have imposed limitations on what they think they can achieve and with that roped off a shot at a very successful life. Limitations are self-defined. We aren't born with them. *Beliefs are learnt behaviour that we pick up over time.* They are your *idea* of what you can and cannot do. And just as they are imposed, they can be lifted.

If you want to be somewhere or be someone, *think* it first.

That is how it starts. With a dream.

The Bare Bones

Life Lessons

From this chapter, you now know that

- Success is, quite literally, all in your head.

- You can succeed despite your genes.

- If you don't try, how will you know what you're genetically predisposed towards?

- Success is made up of three components:

    ○ What you're born with, or **Biology.**

    ○ What you learn along the way, or **Learning.**

    ○ And your deep desire or will to succeed, or **Cognition.**

- By simply changing your approach to problem solving from a *close-ended* to an *open-ended* one, you've opened your mind up to endless possibilities.

- Beliefs are learnt behaviour. And if they can be learnt, they can be unlearnt.

- And finally, success is not out of your league. It is simply out of your comfort zone.

What Do You Do Now?

1 Get a fresh new notebook and start writing down your dreams. A fresh book always signifies a fresh start. And yes, it's better to physically write things down rather than type, as I will explain in the next chapter.

Write down dreams you haven't even dared to think of. Put on paper things that you could have achieved if you were younger, single or not in debt. Think without boundaries, without limitations, without the inconveniences of your current reality.

Be fearless.

Be ambitious.

Be outrageous.

Get in touch with your dreams.

It is the first step.

CHAPTER TWO

The Science of Dreaming

It is a hot, stifling day outside. It is the kind of heat that you know will bring on the monsoon. The cool insides of the operating theatre belie that as I enter, starting off my usual round of surgeries. I look down at my first patient of the day – Sarita, a thirty-four-year-old woman, an investment banker, with three fibroids, a bright woman whom I spoke with during the pre-operative briefing. As per procedure, Sarita is anaesthetized and draped, and the surgical equipment is patiently waiting to be used, gleaming, sterilized and expectant: a laparoscope, 2D cameras, 3D cameras, morcellators, adapters, monitors, light sources, needle holders and diathermy devices and, of course, anaesthesia and suction machines. After a few more checks with the OT nurses to ensure that everything is in place, I'm ready to go.

I like to operate with music. ABBA seems to suggest itself today.

'Mamma Mia, here I go again.'

My little inside joke. Here I go again, performing a fibroid – a benign tumour commonly found in the uterus – removal surgery, medically known as a myomectomy.

I make the first cut.

∽

At this point, you would presumably think that I was in the OT describing an operation I was doing, in the middle of the room, surrounded by instruments and monitors, the team looking on. But I'm not, or rather, that's not where I was. This is just a picture I created in my mind, a technique that prepares me for some of the tougher procedures I do. I thought it up right here. At my clinic. In my room. All in my mind. Using visualization as a technique.

Visualization – defined as the 'formation of mental visual images'[1] – is key to the way I operate, especially the more complex cases. In my mind's eye, I 'see' every little detail of the operation before I perform it, imagining each step of the procedure, the location and size of the incision, the amount of bleeding taking place, as well as the instruments I am using so that I see not only the main event, but all the little steps. I transport myself to the sights and sounds of the theatre. I imagine what I would hear – the beep of the cardiac and respiratory monitors, who I could

---

1 http: http://www.merriam-webster.com/dictionary/visualization; Last Accessed on 17 May 2016

see – my team members, what I would feel – the temperature of the OT, and I also imagine the time I took for the surgery. The more detailed the visualization the better because it recreates the feeling of being there. While the above example is the way I visualize the start of the surgery, I also imagine the procedure right until the very end, or the *outcome*. And I always imagine a successful outcome. I see myself concluding the operation with satisfaction and even end it by thanking my team for a job well done. Because when I actually start my surgery in real time, I get the feeling that I have already been here before and everything seems so much easier. And I *have* been here before. In my head.

While your dream may be to become a pilot, a travel writer, a banker, an actor, a singer, a dancer or a dentist, and while dreaming is a very important step, it is also the first one. Nuttin (1984) has elaborated on the very true fact that 'if you want your dreams to be accomplished, you need to create an image that is both focused (specific) and real (pertaining to your needs)'.[2] This is where visualization comes in. Nuttin also goes on to further state that both 'dreams and visualization…may serve to access those centres in the brain that are directly concerned with taking action'.[3] In order to visualize something, you also need to break down the dream into smaller goals and then visualize those goals, (we will elaborate on that later in the chapter). In other words, before we get into dreams and goals, let's first attempt to understand why visualization is not only important but how your brain supports it.

---

2   Robert E. Franken, *Human Motivation*, 4th ed. VrPacific Grove, CA: Brooks/Cole Pub. Co.,1998

3   Ibd

Greater Chances Of Success = Big Dreams → Audacious Goals → Vivid Visualization → Action

Greater Chances Of Failure = Wishes and Hope → Passivity → No Plan → No Action

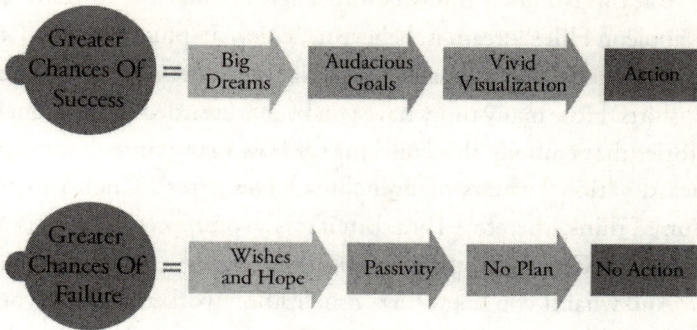

You Can Fool Your Brain

That's right. You heard it here first. **Your brain believes practically anything you tell it.** If you tell it that you are going to lose a match, you probably will. If you tell it that you will never find parking, you probably won't. If you are wearing white and you have convinced your brain that you will come back home with a food stain, it will reward you by ensuring that you're wearing the entire restaurant menu on your return. Good or bad, what you tell your brain often shows itself in reality and what you do see is in most cases what you thought. If your career is, in your opinion, littered with roadblocks and obstacles, then that is what you will probably encounter. But if the road ahead is, according to you, an endless expanse teeming with opportunities, then that is what you will see. Which is why affirmations work so well, why self-help is so powerful, and why the motivational industry is a multi-million-dollar one. Motivational techniques change the way you think with powerful and effective results. You are *taught* the tangible power of believing in yourself even though it was in you all along.

But this isn't new information. There are many renditions of Napoleon Hill's 'dream it, believe it, achieve it' philosophy and it is the subject of countless social media posts, memes, articles and T-shirts. How many times have you been forwarded inspirational stories that embody this concept? Or how many times have you heard various avatars of Frenchman Descartes's Cogito Ergo Sum: I think, therefore I am. But if it is so omnipresent, why is it so absent? Could it be that we *know* this, but don't actually *believe it?* And what if you knew how visualization worked? Would you believe it then? To understand exactly how your brain brilliantly uses this tool, there are two things you need to remember:

First, the process of thinking has actual neurological effects. The brain cannot differentiate between an actual experience *and a powerfully imagined one*. A detailed visualization of a situation fires the *same* brain cells and circuits that will otherwise be used when *actually being in that situation, doing the activity or making the change*. As Robert Cooper says, 'Your brain's prefrontal cortex ... fire(s) up new neural pathways that help you be more successful at making the change.'[4] However, keep in mind that it's a double-edged sword. Visualization works well to create positive outcomes, but it also works equally well to create negative ones. Because the frontal lobe cannot distinguish between 'real failure' and 'imaginary failure',[5] if you keep thinking failure, your emotions

---

4   Robert K. Cooper, *Get Out of Your Own Way: The 5 Keys to Surpassing Everyone's Expectations*, New York: Crown Business, 2006

5   Bobbe L. Sommer and Mark Falstein, *Psycho-Cybernetics 2000*, Englewood Cliffs, New Jersey: Prentice Hall, 1993

start feeling failure and you start making neural circuits that are designed towards failure. And neural circuits – as you read in the chapter 'The Science of Change' – influence your actions. This greatly increases your chances of failing. It all becomes a self-fulfilling prophecy.

Second, visualization is not always active; you don't always have to be visualizing every second of the day. You 'input' your dream or thought, think it up in detail and as you continue with your day, it works on the principle of autopilot. Once you 'take off', you punch in the 'coordinates' for your 'destination' and to that end, 'your automatic mechanism then gives you the technique or methodology to achieve it.'[6] Simply put, when you visualize something, you automatically start thinking in the direction of achieving it and you take concrete action without always realizing it. And there's a reason for this as well: the unconscious activation of your visualized thought stems from your body's Reticular Activating System, or RAS.

To understand how RAS works, let's use the example of sitting in a crowded coffee shop. You have just placed your order for a cup of coffee and the staff behind the counter tells you that they will announce your name to come and collect your drink. You find a place in the coffee shop – excellent, you found a seat near the window – put your bag down, crack open your laptop and start working to fix that loose end in the presentation that's due the next day. The only time you look up is when you hear your name being called out.

But how did you hear your name? The coffee shop was crowded, music was blaring from speakers, a group of school kids

---

6   Ibid

was loudly talking at the next table and all of this was punctuated by the grinding of ice, the mixing of drinks and other orders being called out every few minutes. And you didn't hear a thing. Until the name called out was yours.

You heard your name because of your Reticular Activating System, defined as that 'automatic mechanism inside your brain that brings relevant information to your attention'.[7] Your RAS is almost like a bridge between your conscious and subconscious mind, like a messenger passing on important instructions. In other words, when you constantly think about a message that is important to you, it seeps into your subconscious, waiting to be addressed. You ordered your subconscious mind to listen for your name, and that's why you could hear it. In other words, the RAS can be *programmed* by choosing the right messages to give to your subconscious.

And any message will do. If you're considering buying a Mercedes, for example, and you've always pictured yourself driving a red one, see how much you start noticing a red Mercedes when you're in traffic or standing outside a bar or even doing your errands. From not knowing that they existed, you will start seeing them everywhere because you've programmed your brain into looking out for one.

This is why visualization works so well because the 'path' has been 'navigated'. Targeted visualization also has a term for it: 'psycho-cybernetics', derived from 'psycho', i.e., your psychology and the word 'cybernetics', which are a form of communication. Can you imagine how powerful this is?

---

7   http://www.make-your-goals-happen.com/reticular-activating-system.html; Last Accessed on 17 May 2016

By simply sending the right message to your brain, you are programming it to find the right solutions for you.

It was Napoleon Hill who said that any realistic goal can be achieved by thinking about that goal over and over again. But it is not just Napoleon who climbed that particular hill. Many extremely successful achievers have used visualization as a tool to cross their particular finish lines. Boxing legend Muhammad Ali would claim that he was a world champion even before the game would start. Jim Carrey, the Hollywood superstar, would imagine himself to be the world's greatest actor and even when he was struggling, he'd make a cheque out to himself for one million dollars and sign it. Basketball legend Michael Jordan would always see the last shot in his mind *first,* even before he aimed for the basket in the actual game. In order to achieve your dreams, you would need to provide your brain with the winning result that *you* want. The more vivid the visualization, the more neurons spark to achieve that goal. Keep in mind that targeted visualizations work better than vague ones and that positive, glorious outcomes work better than no outcome at all. In other words: Your visualizations need a strategy too.

The Strategy of Visualization

Is there a technique to visualization? How often should you visualize? To help answer a few questions that surround this technique, I have broken down the process into two parts. The first, **Crafting Visualization**, aims to serve as a guide to help you create targeted thoughts. The second, **Absorbing Visualization**, are some techniques I've learnt that I find helpful when I am visualizing.

I. CRAFTING VISUALIZATION

To help you create detailed and effective visualizations, I came up with a simple formula – GPS. While this may sound like the short form for Global Positioning System, it actually stands for a three-step process to effective visualization:

◉GPS

Goal
Process
Success

Goal. Process. Success – GPS. In that order.
Think of it as a Global Positioning System for your life.

Step One. Break Your Dream Up into Goals.

'The greatest tragedy in life,' a quote often associated with Michelangelo, the sculptor and artist, 'is not that you aim too high and miss it, but that you aim too low and hit it.' Precisely. Why limit your vision? Why not dream as big as you can? **Think of what you want.** It doesn't matter if you have the ability to achieve it or not. Do you want to fly a plane? Be a billionaire? Cure the common cold? Set off that starting gun right here, right now. And while it is normal to think of obstacles when we think of dreams, the problem is that far too often we allow these nagging, negative voices in our heads to out-shout the positive ones.

However, motivational expert Brian Tracy says that dreams are *not* goals and that you need to differentiate between dreams

and goals. The difference between them, to my mind, is that a goal is more *active* and involves a series of actionable steps, whereas a dream is more *passive* where you hope that something happens, but don't take steps to realize your ambition.

Dreams can be short-term or long-term: a ticket to watch a coveted musician could be a dream, getting your first book published could be a dream, winning the Nobel Prize could be a dream. But *how* you get that ticket and *how* you get your book published will be the questions a goal will be able to answer. You therefore have to break your dream up further into goals or *action points*. If your dream is to be a dentist, for example, your goal would be first to get into dental school, but if you're weak in maths, your immediate goal would be to bone up your quantitative skills and get a tutor.

Needless to say, your goals will be limited by your dreams. Which is why you should dream BIG. And in the long-term.

There is a biological reason for dreaming big and in the long-term: your frontal lobe *loves* it, and you will be motivated in the long run if you have a Big Picture to inspire you. If you remember what was discussed in 'The Science of Change', this part of your brain is stimulated by exciting challenges and it thrives under the newness of the obstacles you bring it. Paying attention to what is immediately in front of you in the form of short-term or day-to-day goals – a concept called foot-top gazing[8] – severely

---

8   Robert K. Cooper, *Get Out of Your Own Way: The 5 Keys to Surpassing Everyone's Expectations*, New York: Crown Business, 2006

compromises or may even completely restrict your frontal lobe, whereas looking towards the future 'is a driver of motivation, ingenuity and initiative'.[9] Conducting research on the frontal lobe, neurosurgeon A.R. Luria found that looking beyond your immediate goals and envisioning long-term ones – stretching ahead to five years at the least – activates key areas of the forebrain[10] and is more motivating. **In other words, if you put the long-term ahead of the day-to-day, achieving the long-term may be *much* more motivating.** You can read that again, if you like.

But if you still haven't figured out exactly what you'd like to do, answer the following questions to help you decide what you'd like your dreams to be.

- What does **true success** mean to you?

- When you've achieved your definition of true success, what do you **imagine your life** will look like?

- What needs to **happen** for you to achieve your definition of true success?

- **How** will you know you have attained success?

- How do you think your **family** will respond to your definition of success?

- How does your definition of true success fit in with the **life you have now**?

---

9   Ibid
10   Ibid

Answering these questions may not be easy. Researchers in the field of neuroeconomics have discovered that our brains have a tendency to be overwhelmed by too many choices and because of this we wind up sticking to what we know. So even science agrees that it is not easy for you to find that big fat to-die-for dream, but when you do, it is worth the effort because your life will suddenly be infused with greater meaning.[11]

Once you find your dream, find a way achieve it. *That's* your goal.

Step Two. Break Your Goals Up into Processes. Think of the process, the journey to achieve your goal and mentally rehearse how you will achieve it. In his book, *Evolve Your Brain,* Joe Dispenza uses the term 'mental rehearsal' to describe how best we can use the frontal lobe to change our lives. A rehearsal imitates the experience of the actual process. When we rehearse in great detail, we have lived the experience because, as we know, the brain can't tell the difference between thinking and doing. So, when we actually start to perform the activity for real, we feel like it is something that has already been done before and completion or attainment of that activity seems much easier.

I'll tell you what I mean. If you are the owner of a start-up and you're planning to put a team in place but are new to the process of interviewing, visualize how you will conduct the interview in detail so that you come across as an

11 Robert K. Cooper, *Get Out of Your Own Way: The 5 Keys to Surpassing Everyone's Expectations*, New York: Crown Business, 2006

employer that job seekers can have confidence in. Visualize what you will ask, how you will establish rapport with the candidate, how you will counter difficult questions and so on. You can even visualize how you will be dressed.

Do note, however, that it is hard to rehearse an activity that you have never done before and therefore some knowledge of what you plan to rehearse is absolutely essential. For example, a non-doctor cannot mentally rehearse a surgery. But if you do want to chase a goal that is unfamiliar to you, observe the process before rehearsing. If you have a fear of public speaking but want to speak at your company's annual general meeting, watch other people as they speak on stage. Or, in this age of technology, go online and observe the best of the best perform.

The mental rehearsal process also helps you flag off any errors that you may have not factored in. In *Evolve Your Brain,* Joe Dispenza[12] says that as we begin to think step by step, we encounter a roadblock that challenges our earlier preconceived notions. We start asking questions that challenge our initial assumptions like, 'What would be better?' or 'What if this option were not there?' As Levinson (1978) says, '… as we mature and learn the technique (of visualization), the dream becomes refined and motivationally more powerful.'

The most effective visualization though involves all five senses, says Dr Michael Gervais Ph.D, a performance psychologist in Los Angeles. When imagining the context, what are you seeing, hearing, smelling, touching and tasting? Recreate the environment in which the activity is being performed: don't watch yourself as if you're seeing a movie, but *feel* every scene

---

12 Joe Dispenza, *Evolve Your Brain: The Science of Changing Your Mind,* India: Westland, 2008

there is. For example. if you have to give a speech but are nervous about doing so, first practice your talk in the comfort of your mind. Feel the cool air in the auditorium when you make your speech, hear the silence of the room punctured by the odd cough or the ringing of a cell phone someone forgot to switch off, see the sea of faces partially obscured in the dark; the visualization should be so vivid that it takes almost as long to execute in your vision as it would take in real life.

Step Three. Imagine Victory. This is the last and final step: victory. What kind of end result do you want to achieve? It is not enough just to visualize yourself lacing up your shoes and running a marathon. Once the starting gun goes off, and you are running and keeping pace with the target you have set for yourself, your goal doesn't end there. You need to see yourself cross the finish line with your goal time ticking on. You need to imagine your loved ones standing on the sidelines, calling out your name as you run by. Or if you're so inclined, hordes of screaming people you've never met waving at you as you pass them. Your visualization needs to be so precise that you can almost touch the finish line.

When I visualize my surgeries, I only visualize winning. This doesn't mean that I won't face complications, but this just means that the possibility of my causing surgical errors is minimized because I have imagined the correct steps from start to finish. I have additional confidence going into the surgery since I have convinced my brain that I am a winner. This helps me approach a surgical situation far more calmly because in my mind, I think I have already won.

II. Absorbing Visualization

While Crafting Visualization was one part of the process, Absorbing Visualization is equally integral. You need to constantly 'revisit' your mental pictures and mentally 'rehearse' the process and the outcome until victory is yours.

First, I suggest you put your goals down on paper. Make it a thesis if you have to, but write it down, especially for your bigger goals. I remember reading what Brian Tracy once wrote about goals. He said that if you just write them down, put the paper away and forget about it, reopening the sheet after a while, you'll find that your goals have magically been achieved. Tracy adds that not only should you write your goals down, you should also rewrite them *every day*.

Written goals help awaken feelings of action, persistence and direction. Writing things down also helps in the development of a strategy, and according to Bandura (1991) and Locke and Latham (1990), the process of developing that strategy helps us create the path to the achievement of our goals. This technique crystallizes your thought process beautifully and helps you reaffirm your determination on a daily basis. Writing also helps you take complete responsibility and when we see things in black and white, it suddenly becomes a reality.

Writing things down is *that* powerful.

Second, get a room. Spend some time with yourself once a day reading what you have written, visualizing how you will achieve the goals (the process) and how you will succeed (the outcome). I find that a quiet room and a designated time for visualization – say early in the morning – really help. By repeating the process over and over again, you're sending a stronger message to your subconscious through your RAS. You're punching in the coordinates for your final destination on a day-to-day basis.

And every day takes you closer and closer to your goal.

The Bare Bones

Life Lessons

From this chapter, you now know that

- Your brain believes anything you tell it.

- What message you want to send out to your brain depends entirely on you.

- Your brain cannot tell the difference between an actual experience and a vividly imagined one.

- The unconscious activation of your visualized thoughts stems from your body's RAS. In other words, your brain is designed to respond extremely well to visualization.

- Long-term goals are more motivating than short-term goals and stimulate your frontal lobe. Think at least five years into the future.

- Design the visualization of your goals using the GPS approach:

  - **Goal**: The tangible, actionable aspects of your dreams.

  - **Process**: How you will achieve it.

  - **Success**: How you imagine winning.

- Write your goals down every day and visualize the process and your success at achieving the goal.

WHAT DO YOU DO NOW?

2 **Make your dreams tangible by using the GPS approach.** First, after writing your dreams, convert them into tangible goals. Second, isolate a time in the day for you to visualize the goal, the process and the success of these. Third, rewrite your goals every day and continue to do so until you achieve them. Because achieve them you will.

Part Two

THE LEARNING COMPONENT

CHAPTER THREE

Unlearn

Can the ghosts haunting your career be exorcised?
If what you are currently doing is hampering your
growth, can what has already been learnt – over
perhaps decades – be *unlearnt*? And by unlearning,
can we make way for learning anew? But how do
you change trajectories? How do you get on to a
new path? That the brain can do it – 'The Science
of Change' teaches us it can – but can *you*? If
the anatomy of success really is within you, what
prevents you from changing the course of your
career, and therefore your life? In other words, how
do you learn a new language, the language of success?

Before we get into lessons that we can imbibe from the medical profession, it is important to first understand that to be all you can be, not only will you have to unlearn bad work habits and re-learn new ones, but you also have to change the way you think about learning itself. One of the best things I have ever read was what Benjamin Barber once said about learning. He said there are only two kinds of people in this world: not the rich and the poor or not the educated and the uneducated; the world is simply divided into learners and non-learners. And the successful ones are the ones who learn.

There's nothing wrong with admitting that you lack a certain skill or need help in an area you are weak in. You're never too old to ask questions and you're never too old to raise your hand. But while Benjamin Barber claimed that learners will inherit the earth, I'd like to take this thought a little further. I'd like to differentiate not between the learners and the non-learners – because in medicine, as with many other careers, pretty much everyone has to be a learner – but between the *attitudes* towards learning I believe the *good* learners will inherit the earth, i.e., those who are *receptive* to learning. And not everyone is a *good* learner. I see that all the time.

Carol Dweck, in her seminal, ground-breaking book *Mindset*, postulates the idea that people are of two kinds: those with a **fixed** mindset and those with a **growth** mindset. The fixed mindset believes that their intelligence, talent and other attributes are fixed, that they cannot be changed and good or bad, they are bound by what they are born with. The growth mindset, on the other hand, believes that attributes can be acquired and intelligence can be increased. Those in possession of the growth mindset believe that talents, if not immediately present or inherited, can be nurtured, heightened and developed.

Dweck goes on to further elaborate the consequences of both mindsets. Fixed mindsets are sensitive to criticism and spend their lives trying to prove how intelligent, talented or special they are. They also, she concludes, have a tendency to believe they are superior.

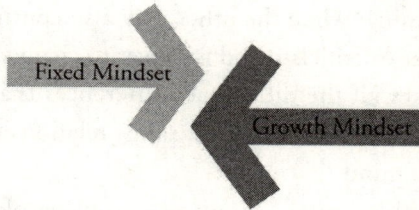

Fixed Mindset

Growth Mindset

The Two Kinds of Mindsets: Carol Dweck

They are closed to new ideas and like to surround themselves with yes-men: those who approve their ideas and those who agree with them without – or very little – exception. Growth mindsets, on the other hand, don't believe in their essential superiority, are not taken with their inherited gifts, want to create and work in atmospheres that are growth-oriented and they have the courage to admit the skills they do not have and work towards acquiring them if needed. Which is not to say that those with fixed mindsets don't go on to become CEOs, sportsmen and celebrities; they do. But have they truly done all they are capable of? And how long will they be able to stay at the top before they become their own enemy?

Which one reminds you of you?

I'll try and elaborate what Dweck meant by using my own real-life experiences with training surgeons. As a laparoscopic surgeon who also trains doctors at the Center of Excellence for Minimal Access Surgery Training (CeMAST), I have come to better understand – over the course of many years – which doctors will make waves during their careers and which ones will run the risk of never being able to exploit their potential. The difference between these two kinds of doctors? One wishes to continue learning, while the other may also continue learning, but is resistant to criticism and is slower to change. This crucial variance makes all the difference: differences that, over time, may affect their careers, finances, skills, relationships and even their peace of mind.

Let's take the case of Dr Advait – a gynaecologist with an interest in laparoscopy, or minimal invasive surgery, and Dr Bhavna – also a fresh medical postgraduate who is interested in the same field. They both came in within a week of each other to train with me, both eager to learn. But soon enough, I was able to tell how their careers would progress.

Advait topped medical school. All his life, he topped virtually every class, exam and course and flew into medical school. Bhavna's journey into medicine could be described as more of a struggle. Nearly tanking her science exams in the seventh standard, the realization that her dream of becoming a doctor was quite simply linked to her performance in science made her more determined to work harder and achieve her goal. Bhavna's parents got a tutor to train her and she worked her way up, turning bad grades into good ones, better for the experience. Bhavna knew what failure tasted like. Advait did not.

When they started hitting roadblocks in their training, I realized that Advait was sensitive to being told he needed further training in suturing skills. He spent his time going on the defensive and though he dutifully followed my instructions and put in the work, I got the impression he was only doing it to get another gold star and prove to me how smart he was; like he always did. Bhavna, on the other hand, was not attaching too much importance to her immediate setbacks but was placing them in a wider context. Everything she did was not so much to get my approval, but was more geared towards the larger purpose of improving the quality of the lives of her patients. *She learnt for the long term.* She wouldn't fuss over small chidings and minor mistakes. Over time, Bhavna's eagerness only grew. Advait, on the other hand, was happy so long as he made me – his instructor – happy. Why wouldn't he be when he could get another gold star? I knew then that Advait may not make a great doctor. He'd be a good doctor, yes. But Bhavna would get more gold stars in the overall tally. Over the course of her career, when it really counted.

Inside the Line

'Inside the Line' learners are like Advait. They have, like Carol Dweck says, an idea of their fixed intelligence. They are sensitive to criticism, are reluctant to change and will only take on things that they think they can excel at. They get bored with what they don't understand or are not immediately good at. They constantly seek validation and in that struggle, attempt things that hover around their comfort zone. I call it 'Inside the Line' because it is an invisible line, one which they have drawn around themselves and have used to define them.

Outside the Line

'Outside the Line' learners don't even know that there is a line to be drawn. They are neither too encouraged by a good outcome nor too discouraged by a bad one. Because they are able to separate themselves from the task and don't invest all their self-esteem in the failure or success of their work, they keep defying expectations as they don't spend time seeking validation, either from themselves or others. They are far more likely to take unsuccessful risks, but they don't let failure wound them. No pain, no gain. No guts, no glory. 'Outside the Line' learners have a growth mindset. They are eager to learn, even at the cost of people laughing at them or criticizing them.

However, people don't usually fall into a particular category, but are a mix of the two. To go back to Dweck, people can have both fixed *and* growth mindsets, depending on the context. You can have a fixed mindset about your work, but a growth mindset about your relationships, or vice versa. The good news is that attitudes towards learning can change by just believing they can. Learning is a type of behaviour that in itself can be *learnt*. All learning asks of you is that you learn how to learn. And that is really one of the points of both the book and the chapter: to convince you that we are biologically predisposed to succeed, that skills can be picked up and that no matter where you are, you are on the learning continuum. You can still – with the right attitude towards your environment – get there. Because mindsets can change from fixed to growth, from limit to limitless, from fear to fearless.

What do you want to become? Where do you want to be?

How Much Is Too Much?

While learning itself is important, how you *organize* your learning is also incredibly crucial. Paradoxically, the journey to limitless possibilities is to set smaller limits, breaking the task down into less intimidating and more achievable bits. Noel Tichy, a professor at Michigan Business School, writes about the comfort zone and about what is beyond. He believes that in order to expand your comfort zone, you need to gently push out the circle, expanding your idea of what you can do one limit at a time.

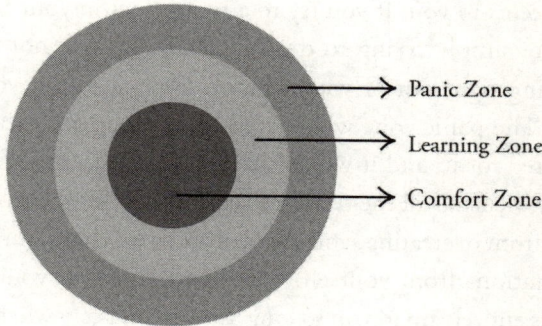

$$\longrightarrow \text{Panic Zone}$$
$$\longrightarrow \text{Learning Zone}$$
$$\longrightarrow \text{Comfort Zone}$$

The Comfort Zone: Noel Tichy

Your comfort zone, needless to say, is where you currently are. It is the sphere within which you operate and there is an invisible border over which you do not step. This comforts you but also limits you at the same time. Your learning zone is that which is just outside your comfort zone and which defines the area of new experiences that are slightly – but not totally – alien to you. The panic zone is so outside your comfort zone that it may as well be on another planet. You can't identify with the panic zone if you are viewing it from your vantage point, safely ensconced in your comfort zone. Learning is all about getting out of your comfort zone as no progress can be made within the comfort zone. Success lies outside the comfort zone.

To translate this abstract theory into action, let's say your comfort zone for exercise is a brisk walk every morning. You now want to run a marathon, but you currently have the ability to walk only a few kilometres at a time. First day on the running track you see someone whizz past you at the speed of light, or so it seems to you. If you try to attempt that in your first week, you are simply trying to do something you are not ready to, zooming right out of your comfort zone and into your panic zone. The panic zone will overwhelm you because you are not prepared for it, and it will ensure that you don't succeed. That is why diets fail all the time: you attempt to do too much at one time; from overeating, you suddenly starve or have unreasonable expectations from yourself. What you define as your learning zone is entirely up to you so long as you don't stay where you are.

Transforming your life and your career is a process of incremental change. You need to continually absorb skills by moving out of your comfort zone a little bit at a time, setting new goals. You know you've made progress when your learning zone becomes your new comfort zone.

Biologically, learning is nothing but the ability to create and develop goal-oriented neural networks; in other words, an orchestrated neural symphony.[1] Your brain – in a process called neuroplasticity – has the ability to re-wire and create new

---

1   Joe Dispenza, *Evolve Your Brain: The Science of Changing Your Mind*, India: Westland, 2008

networks for new things and with the right training, the right direction and with the right intention, you can learn almost anything at nearly any age. And you can be really good at it, too.

Malcolm Gladwell, in his book *Blink*, has quoted Daniel Levitan when he says that it takes 10,000 hours to achieve mastery over anything, depending on what you're learning and if you have 10,000 hours to spare. What's 10,000 hours in the course of a working lifetime which has approximately 1,00,000 working hours? As was once said, *learning is experience, all else is commentary*. In other words, one of the most powerful ways of learning is through actually doing it, not talking about it. If that isn't powerful, I don't know what is.

The ensuing pages will give you a glimpse of what you can absorb from how doctors learn, how they think and how they make mistakes. The second part of this book will teach you just how to get new experiences and relearn new ways to work, thereby stimulating your frontal lobe – the big daddy of change. But what lessons can non-doctors learn from doctors? Plenty, in fact. Because doctors are trained to save human lives, when the stakes are the highest and the learning curve to save them is the steepest. And maybe by understanding how they learn to heal and the decisions they have to take, you can begin to draw comparisons to your own career, thereby healing, redirecting and mending your own trajectories. If you've dreamt the dream, set your target and pitched the tent, what's keeping you in the rut? If mediocrity is a habit, challenge mediocrity. If lethargy is a habit, challenge lethargy. If pessimism is a habit, challenge pessimism.

It can all be done.

Or rather, it can all be learnt.

CHAPTER FOUR

Lessons Learnt from Medical Rigour

'Why did this happen, Doctor? It doesn't run in our family.'
'Malignant? Am I going to die?'
'Can you save me?'

There comes a time in your medical career when you are almost as stumped as your patient. When patients' medical reports suddenly throw up something no doctor expected, there comes a point when you are faced with the simple truth about the human body: not only is it a great leveller, it is also a great mystery. Patients see doctors as god-like figures, as mortals with expectations of delivering immortality. I wish I had the answer to every disease, to pain, to unimaginable suffering, but I don't. When patients ask me why they have been diagnosed with fibroids or whether they will get them again, I don't have an answer. There is even a medical term for conditions or diseases with no known cause: *idiopathic*. Idiopathic. A Latin word for shrugging your shoulders.

56

It is my belief that medicine, without exception, is the hardest profession there is. And I speak in absolute terms. Not 'probably the hardest' or 'one of the hardest', it *is* the hardest profession there is. I say this with confidence not because I am a surgeon myself or because I have trained for many years, but because medicine is the only profession that has the direct, applied ability to save a human life. And to be responsible for someone's life, to have a near complete stranger place their trust in you with the *most* important thing to *them*; what can be the hardest thing in life than life itself? But while being a doctor can be a tremendous privilege, it can also be the most intimidating and frightening experience since exceptional power brings with it exceptional responsibility. An operating surgeon is a lonely professional because, as Paul Ruggieri in his book *Confessions of an ER Surgeon* puts it, 'For me, the corridor leading into the operation room is a long, lonely one, the path to a place where I am responsible for all that happens, the good, the bad and the ugly.'

And it can truly get very ugly. Surgical or medical cases are not always open-and-shut ones. An ultrasound, for example, can show that the patient has one large fibroid. But when I operate on the same patient and insert a telescope, the fibroid looks degenerated with the possibility of cancer. Or suddenly in the middle of surgery, a patient like Meera could be found to have deep, embedded scar tissue on her uterus, making it extremely hard to deliver a baby. What goes on inside our bodies is a mystery; and mysteries like to play hide-and-seek. What do you do when all your training, all your homework, all your work with a patient prepares you for one thing, but you see another?

You adapt. And quickly. In terms of the brain, this process is called 'cognitive flexibility'. It enables a person to quickly change course. And that is what doctors and surgeons are trained to do. They are trained to react fast and are compelled to work with the same accuracy whether they are fresh from a good night's sleep or brutally sleep-deprived. This is why medical training deliberately subjects doctors to gruelling hours, lack of sleep and sometimes even the absence of good nutrition since only those who have the ability to work under tremendous pressure are truly qualified to go to the next level.

So what is the correlation between those who are trained to save lives and those who aren't? And what can you learn from them? I can give you a magical shortcut to answering this question: an answer that is as simple as it is irrefutable.

And the shortcut to answering this is that there aren't any shortcuts.

There are no shortcuts to becoming and being something *good*. The sooner it is understood, the better and more successful your life will be. And if this is the first and only lesson you get from this book, I'll consider my job done. Having said that, there are tons of cheat sheets which will happily put you on the path to mediocrity. But I have to then ask the question I asked in the beginning of this book: are you okay with being okay?

The second reason I opened 'Part Two' with this chapter and why I bring this to you is that medicine has a set, standardized way to learn. It has a set practice. And unless you are a child prodigy, everyone takes around the same amount of time to become a doctor. From theory to the practical, the journey from the basics to finally treating a patient becomes something you *earn,* the ultimate citadel and the ultimate prize. So what else can we learn from how doctors are trained?

Apprenticeship.

From them we can learn how to learn.

This is not to say that other professions aren't equally daunting from a training perspective, and there is no doubt there are some commonalities between medicine and other educational streams, but there are ways medicine harshly initiates you into your working life that few careers do. It is an incredibly daunting achievement to get into medical school itself. As of 2015, over 6,00,000 students appeared for medical entrance tests, vying for a little over 50,000 seats.[1] From textbooks and theory, medical students are catapulted into a world of cadavers, organs, blood, tissue and intestines. They poke through brain tissue, nerves, arteries, muscles, ligaments and joints. Some students faint and many drop out, this first stage already becoming a natural selection process. Eighteen months of dissecting heads, necks, thoraxes, abdomens, upper extremities, lower extremities and another eighteen months understanding cells and why they go bad in pathology. This is followed by the study of pharmacology – drugs and their composition – and other related medical subjects. Medical studies are fuelled by coffee, late nights, exams and the feeling that you aren't and will never be good enough.

Four years of this and you still haven't treated a single patient. The practical internships start in the fifth and final year, exposing interns to working in hospitals in a multitude of departments like general surgery, medicine, gynaecology, obstetrics, preventive and social medicine, ophthalmology, orthopaedics, paediatrics

---

1   http://timesofindia.indiatimes.com/home/education/
    entrance-exams/99-4-of-all-candidates-fail-AIPMT-every-year/
    articleshow/47683394.cms; Last Accessed on 18 May 2016

and then subjecting them to more sleeplessness and the belief that if they sleep on their night rounds, the patient will die and they will be responsible. Doctors train under all kinds of terror.

If you *do* get a postgraduate seat in the specialty of your choice, three more years of training await you. You become a junior resident, a house officer, you live in dormitories, share rooms, sleep on floors and work continuously, sometimes even for forty-eight hours at a stretch. No food, no sleep and no rest. Because lives are at stake. Trainee surgeons are assigned a unit which constitutes two resident officers, a registrar, a lecturer, two associate professors and one professor. You begin by doing menial tasks like filling in forms, filling in several registers and papers. You collect blood for various tests, just keep taking pre-operative and post-operative rounds. Lots of wounds need dressing – you are in charge. It is only when you complete your internship that you receive your graduation degree which certifies you to see patients and start your own independent general practice.

And this is just graduation. While you are doing your postgraduate training, which takes another three years, you are required to simultaneously prepare for your masters exams. MS and MD are highly coveted degrees. Once you clear these, you have the licence to perform surgeries on your own. And this doesn't even include surgical techniques like advanced laparoscopy.

But this is where it gets interesting. As an intern or a junior resident, doctors broadly employ three techniques of learning: learning by observation, learning by deliberate practice and learning by breaking it down. The first, learning by observation, employs mirror neurons in your brain. But what are these mirror neurons and why are they so important?

Technique One | Learning by Observation

In the nineties, at Giacomo Rizzolatti's private laboratory in Italy, a team of neuroscientists unearthed the concept of mirror neurons while studying the brains of monkeys. What was discovered was unbelievable. The scientists found that the *same* motor command neurons fire when an action is done – like picking up a banana or getting a peanut – as when that action is *observed* by other monkeys watching these actions being performed. This meant that these primates would experience a similar sensation in both doing and observing the same activity, allowing them to put themselves in place of another and perceive its movements as if they were doing them. These motor command neurons are called 'mirror neurons' which, in other words, means that

Seeing is almost as good as doing.

Medical students observe for *years* before they are allowed to treat patients. Observing is one of the best ways to learn. The most important thing to do is choose a good mentor, ideally someone who can do good work, if not brilliant. Medical students have been known to change their jobs, cities and even countries, all for that one chance to work with the best of the best.

When you want to get ahead, it may be crucial to choose someone who has the skills that you want to learn. It needn't always be technical skills. If you admire someone's ability to close a sale or lead a new team or think on their feet, push, push and push some more to work with them. Be fastidious about who you choose to observe because they could be as good as *you* get. And try to focus on choosing people who have the ability to also impart useful, critical feedback. The second pillar of learning anything new is acting on feedback through the process of 'deliberate practice'.

Technique Two | Learning by Deliberate Practice

Deliberate practice, according to K. Anders Ericsson and his team, is a feedback-led method designed to improve performance. 'Deliberate' = targeted feedback and 'Practice' = incorporating the feedback while practising. In other words, based on constructive criticism, you practise, practise and practise.

Deliberate practice has a few hallmarks:

1. You need a good coach who has the ability to teach.
2. The process involves repetition, i.e., practising the same thing over and over again.
3. Feedback is required, both positive and negative.
4. It is demanding and requires intense focus.
5. It is hard and not always fun.

Irrespective of seniority, doctors are in a constant state of deliberate practice. They are working on feedback all the time because they are surrounded by it – feedback from patients, from other doctors and sometimes from nurses and technicians, too. Because of the ever-evolving nature of medicine – new discoveries and new medical techniques emerging all the time – they need to constantly work on themselves. Being open to feedback is vital for career survival. But even with deliberate practice, it is important to pay heed to Noel Tichy's concentric model of learning {refer to page 53}. It is important to identify your learning zone and practise in that zone itself. It takes wisdom to understand which is which.

It doesn't matter where you are on your career trajectory, you still need a coach or a mentor who can take your work to the next level because even if you are at the top of your game, there's always room for improvement. Top sports stars, musicians and surgeons practise all the time. They are *always* in their learning zone because they know that if they stay in their comfort zone, they will get left behind. Their performances are controlled and conscious but not automatic or robotic. Deliberate practice should also not be confused with mere activity: it is about quality of practice, about making new neural connections, measured in terms of how much progress you have made and *not* about how many hours you've spent on it. Having said that, if it is a particularly challenging skill, practise as often as you can.

Technique Three | Learning by Breaking It Down

I am a laparoscopic surgeon, specializing in hysterectomies and myomas (fibroids). For those unfamiliar with the term, laparoscopy is a minimal invasive operating technique which enables surgeons to deliver the same results without making large cuts on the body, thereby reducing the risk of post-operative infection, complications and drastically reducing the time taken to heal. And, of course, eliminating the occurrence of big, unsightly scars. Right now, technology has made it possible to perform cholecystectomies (gall bladder), hysterectomies (uterus), appendectomies (appendix), bariatric (weight reduction) surgery and myomectomies (fibroids) laparoscopically even as more and more specialties open up. But even for trained open surgeons, laparoscopy is a whole new ball game because they come in with a completely different understanding of how to operate.

The credo of Mumbai's Centre of Excellence for Minimal Access Surgery Training (CeMAST) is to train surgeons in laparoscopy. This training is imparted to already-trained surgeons who have some experience in open surgery, i.e., where they cut the body open to reveal – and fully expose – the area/organ that needs surgery. How we train surgeons at CeMAST is the third technique I wanted to discuss.

Here, one of the main skills I teach surgeons – laparoscopic suturing – is broken down into smaller sub-activities using a method called neuro linguistic programming (NLP) where big activities are 'chunked' down into smaller sub-activities. Doctors are encouraged to practise and excel at the sub-activities first and then put it all together to perform the activity as a whole. From one big mountain, learners now climb smaller hills, one hill at a time. As a trained NLP practitioner myself, I find that imparting training in this way demystifies the activity almost immediately and any process, no matter how complicated, seems a lot less intimidating now.

Since laparoscopy is about hand-eye coordination, the training process starts with using surgical instruments to lift and sort coloured beads. It sounds simple enough, but when the beads are enclosed in a simulator and you have to reach them in an enclosed glass case, it becomes much harder. Immediately, you are far more immobilized and you lose your orientation a lot more than if you were performing surgery on what was directly in front of you. You have to perform multiple hand-eye coordination tasks within the glass case that test your dexterity, right from picking up and sorting the beads as per colour to stacking mints (with holes in them) on a toothpick. The next stage involves practising suturing on animal cadavers and even this is broken down into multiple little steps; right from picking up the needle to finally practising how to tie a surgical knot, which in itself is also divided into four stages. All of the above are practised separately and also together. Just to practise *one* surgical knot.

Laparoscopic Dexterity Training

There is no activity too intimidating which cannot be made approachable by breaking it down. You may not be medically permitted to suture, but you can be taught. Even trained surgeons coming in to learn suturing techniques would wonder how to do it. But when the activity was broken down, it led to a whole new world of understanding.

By pushing yourself, by practising and by using smart learning techniques you can learn almost anything. And you can find alternative means to learn as well. Observation, for example, doesn't always have to be done in person; it can be done through videos – we are Internet monkeys after all. But whatever you do, understand that, like the German philosopher Goethe said, 'Everything is hard before it is easy.' Learning something new is not enjoyable. It is difficult and painful, and includes long hours, falling down and bruising your ego, and picking yourself up again. Getting better is not as much about talent as it is about resilience. The best surgeons are not always the most intelligent, but they are the ones who are the most driven. The best surgeons are the ones who practise.

It is important to know that you will make mistakes, but it is even more important to know that you have to inculcate the ability, and the heart, to get over them. Don't expect to magically improve overnight. Look out instead for small, incremental improvements on a daily basis. That is how you will know you are getting better. As your skills in an activity improve, so does your efficiency; this gives you the potential to be on top of your game. And at the top of your career.

What Juggling Taught Me

A seminar with Vanda North – the founder and director of The Learning Consortium – in 1999 was my first introduction to juggling. Since then, I've been hooked. It is now a part of my motivational talks and I always ask audience members to try it. I'm even surprised at times by how responsive and excited the audience gets. While I use it to illustrate how to get more balance in life, I would like to use it here for another reason: juggling teaches you so many more things. It is an excellent metaphor for the art of learning. And in the process, you learn a little bit about yourself too.

To learn juggling, you start with one ball, throwing it up with one hand and catching it with the other. When you're comfortable, add the second ball. Throw the two balls up one after the other. Then, throw each ball to a particular height in staggered timing. Catch them as they fall into your opposing palms. When you are at ease with this, add the third. Three-ball juggling requires time, determination and patience. And a lot of it. In between dropping the ball and picking it up again and again, and driving myself insane in the process, I picked up a few other lessons along the way:

Juggling teaches you that 'by stretching yourself beyond your perceived level of competence you accelerate your development of competence'.[2] When you first started practising, you never imagined you would be able to do it. But when you push yourself, you suddenly realize that you have raced past your own expectations. You get a feeling that if you learn to juggle, if you learn to do something you originally associated with something only 'other' people were capable of, you can learn just about anything you put your mind to.

Juggling teaches you how to relax and focus at the same time.[3] To a doctor, this skill is especially integral as it transports you to a new state of relaxed concentration, essential for surgery and essential for high performance in any field of work.

Juggling teaches you that a good way to learn is to break down a task into smaller pieces. Instead of tackling one big mountain, first learn to climb smaller hills.

---

2   Michael Gelb and Tony Buzan, *Lessons from the Art of Juggling: How to Achieve Your Full Potential in Business, Learning, and Life,* New York: Harmony Books, 1994

3   Ibid

Juggling teaches you that things get harder in the beginning, but it gets easier as you go along. And nothing works right the first time.

Juggling gives you a ringside seat to your own improvement. You can see yourself getting better.

Juggling teaches you that the greater the difficulty, the greater the challenge. But the greater the challenge, the greater the reward.

But the most important lesson of them all is it teaches you that if you drop the ball, all you have to do to get back on track is to pick it up. All you have to do is forget the past, move on and focus on mastering the skill in front of you. As W. Somerset Maugham once said, 'It's a funny thing about life; if you refuse to accept anything but the best, you very often get it.'[4]

THE STAGES OF LEARNING
WILLIAM HOWELL'S CONSCIOUS COMPETENCE MODEL

William Howell's 'Conscious Competence Model' is a path-breaking analysis of the journey of a learner. He says that learning moves in four steps. The first stage, Unconscious Incompetence, is when you don't know that you don't know a particular skill or function. Once you know that you don't know a skill, that stage is called Conscious Incompetence. This will propel you into Conscious Competence, where you work deliberately and slowly on developing your skills: this is where you

---

4   http://www.brainyquote.com/quotes/quotes/w/wsomerset110037.
html; Last Accessed on 16 May 2016

use your frontal lobe and become consciously better at what you do. And finally, you move into Unconscious Competence, where you are so skilled that you start doing this automatically, where your excellence becomes a habit. In addition to this, I've come up with a stage called Unconscious Supercompetence, where you become brilliant over time without even being aware of it. Sportsmen like Sachin Tendulkar, Abhinav Bindra and Viswanathan Anand would fall into this category.

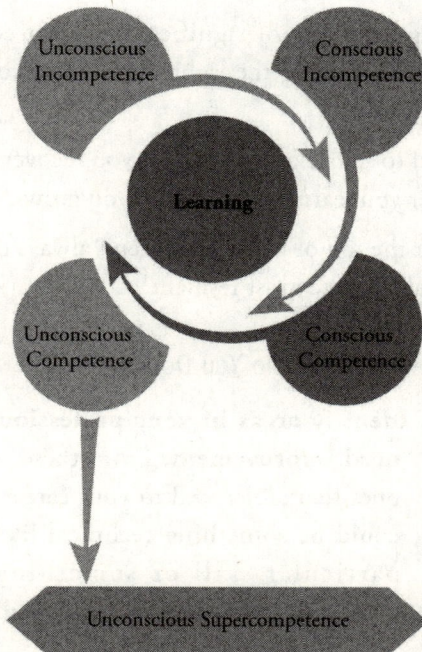

The Bare Bones

Life Lessons

From this chapter, you now know that

- To achieve anything of value and greatness, there are no shortcuts.

- There are three main techniques that doctors use:

  o   Learning by Observation

  o   Learning by Deliberate Practice

  o   Learning by Breaking It Down

- Learning anything of significance is not easy, but by practising and using the right techniques, you can learn almost anything.

- Get used to setbacks; the quicker you recover from them, the faster you learn and the faster you grow.

- Those at the top of their fields aren't always the smartest, but are always the most resilient.

What Do You Do Now?

3 **Identify areas in your professional life that need improvement.** From these, shortlist the ones that are crucial to your career growth – it could be something technical like learning a particular skill or something soft like communication or negotiation skills. Next, see how you can improve using the three learning techniques and who can help you with them: could you find someone you can observe? Or someone who has a flair for teaching you by breaking down the technique into smaller parts? Or, simply, could you identify someone who can be honest with you and give you feedback where you most need it?

CHAPTER FIVE

The Pursuit of Mastery

You are a thirty-one-year-old woman. After two decades of wearing contact lenses, you have decided to take the plunge and opt for LASIK eye surgery to get rid of your glasses once and for all. But since this is such a big decision, you take your time to make it. You do your reading, you ask around and you eventually wind up shortlisting two surgeons for the job. After some more research, you have been told that one of them is just about average and one of them is excellent, the best in the business. All else being equal, which one would you choose? What would your answer be?

Seems like a fairly simple choice, a no-brainer if you like. Most people will choose the doctor with excellent recommendations. No one, if given a choice, would ever settle for someone average and along the course of any career, preference will always be given to someone who has achieved mastery over their skills.

But what is this mastery that we talk about? For the purpose of this chapter, mastery is defined in terms of 'outstanding skill', 'expertise' or 'full command or understanding of a subject',[1] indicating a certain superiority over both an area and, implicitly within it, over others in the same domain. Mastery is concerned with the acquisition of knowledge and the development of skills. When you master something, your learning is complete in that subject or skill; you know everything there is to know. The purpose of mastery is to ensure complete competence and that competence is further broken down into skill, capacity, ability, fitness and proficiency. Henry Murray, a motivational expert, further defined the need to achieve mastery so as to 'observe obstacles, to exercise power, to strive to do something difficult'.

But is mastery necessary?

If you stay in the same place long enough, you get good – if not brilliant – over time. But the *pursuit of mastery* is not about staying in the same place.

It is about going places.

The payoff to being a master of your domain is high, right from getting plum projects and high-profile roles to the financial implications of being at the top of your game. To be known for your mastery over something is also a matter of great prestige and will open doors and speak for you, too.

---

1   http://www.thefreedictionary.com/mastery; Last Accessed on 16 May 2016

The pursuit of mastery is also an extremely personal one. Aspiring to reach the ultimate level of expertise is an ambition in itself, aside from making money or making it to the top of your company, for example. It may or may not be what you want to do. Like any ambition you set for yourself, it is voluntary; just because you have learnt something, it doesn't necessarily mean you need to master it.

Or should you?

I find in my experience that people greatly underestimate how good other people are in their own skill sets and put down their competitor's career progression to softer issues like managing work politics or, in the case of doctors, a better bedside manner, a better referral network or plain and simple luck. Maybe the reason they are climbing up the ladder is because they have not managed to understand the 'system'. Maybe it is not just luck.

Maybe they are just better at what they do.

Mastery is not necessarily restricted to a skill. You could have knowledge-based mastery where, as a lawyer for example, you have complete command over the subject matter – like a particular section of the law. You could also have skill-based mastery like laparoscopic surgery which enables you to operate without making large incisions. You can also master a process, like understanding the way your company manages their supply chain. Inherent in the definition of mastery is being extremely proficient in that specialty.

For hundreds of years, it was believed that mastery was nothing but inexplicable genius, within the reach of only a genetically privileged few.[2] The talent that people seemed to

---

2   Robert Greene, *Mastery*, London: Profile, 2012

display was seen as inborn or just luck. While we have attempted to deconstruct this myth in the previous chapters, there is a story I remember reading that I wanted to share with you. Known to all as a child prodigy, composer Wolfgang Amadeus Mozart apparently composed his first piece on the violin at the age of five and by the age of ten[3] had many full works to his name. Regarded as a genius, he composed his *'Piano Concerto Number 9'* at the age of twenty-one. To this day, it is thought of as a masterpiece.

Were his achievements inexplicable? Was his genius unaccounted for? Was he just born this way? In *Genius Explained*, Michael Howe, a psychologist at the University of Exeter, UK, estimated that even before turning six, Mozart had practised for an unbelievable 3,500 hours. Mozart's father, Leopold Mozart, was a performer, composer and acclaimed teacher; the year Wolfgang was born was the same year his book on violin instruction was published. But he was also a parent who pushed young Wolfgang into music, training him in composition and performance from the age of three. Not only did Wolfgang practise, but he *deliberately* practised because he was living with his teacher. *'Piano Concerto Number 9'* emerged not out of thin air but as the result of *eighteen years* of focused practice and training.

Not so inexplicable after all.

Even if there are genetic factors in play, it takes a very special effort to become better than good. To be the best. To be all you can be. As Paul Arden says, *'Everyone wants to be good, but not many are prepared to make the sacrifices it takes to be great.'* And

---

3   Matthew Syed, *Bounce: How Champions Are Made*, London: Fourth Estate, 2010

it *does* take sacrifice. To excel at something requires resources, practice and some pretty unshakeable faith in yourself. It requires time away from friends, family, from yourself and sometimes even from work itself even though, ironically, that is why you are trying to master it. Most people underestimate how long it takes to be excellent at something.

When you are learning new skills, the brain is packed with new information and a lot of frenetic activity is going on because neural circuits are being created and rewired. But these circuits are still new and raw, and need to become hardwired before you can perform that skill with ease. The process of hardwiring circuits takes time because it is a function of repeat practice, feedback and fine-tuning based on that feedback. After the circuits are hardwired, the performance of that skill becomes 'automatic' to you and the activity is performed from another part of the brain where it remains. This is also popularly referred to as 'muscle memory'.

Reaching this level of automaticity requires hours and hours of practice. According to neuroscientist Daniel Levitan, *'The amount of quality practice you need to achieve mastery in any field is 10,000 hours.'* 10,000 hours, or ten years of practice four hours a day, or five years of practice at eight hours a day seems to apply to everyone from athletes to musicians to writers to chess players and even to surgeons. And while it sounds daunting, this would probably be what a mid-career professional in his thirties or forties would have acquired if he or she were working on the same skill set for over ten years of their career. In terms of the process of achieving mastery, there is no mystery. It is on the same continuum as when you are learning something, except what elevates you to the next level and enables you to achieve mastery is:

Deliberate Practice.

Because it is not just how much you practise, it is also how *well* you practise.

To master something, you must never stop learning. You stick with the area you want to excel in, continually absorb feedback, deliberately and consistently practise and never stop practising. In order to truly achieve mastery over a field, you must also love the subject: it is best not to look for approval or validation – if you want to do it, do it for yourself. First, be willing to accept challenges that will help you grow, toughen you up and enable you to transform. Second, try and master only one skill at a time.[4] When I learnt laparoscopic surgery, I first learnt to do laparoscopic suturing which, if not done correctly, is one of the biggest roadblocks to being a good laparoscopic surgeon. It was only then that I worked on other signature skills. But irrespective of what you choose, find the right teacher. A bad teacher can set you back years. Find a mentor who will be invested in your progress and is able to give you constructive feedback. Find a teacher who is selfless and fair in their evaluation and has your best interests at heart. The road to mastery requires clarity, focus, discipline, observation and persistence.

There is a reason why it is called a pursuit of mastery. You have to chase it, it won't chase you.

However, even during your journey there may come a time when you will experience boredom or an obstacle in your training which will make you want to give up. Even though making those

---

4   Robert Greene, *Mastery*, London: Profile, 2012

kinds of sacrifices is not everyone's cup of tea, if you *aren't* motivated to get to the next level, it is important to reflect on the reason.

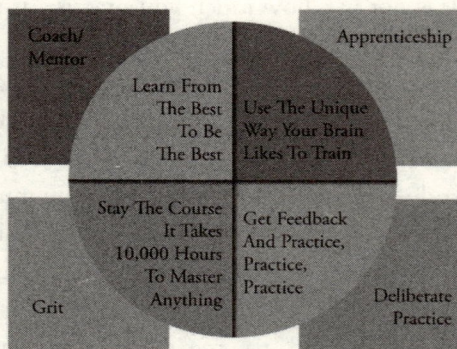

What it Takes to Achieve Mastery

Why do we give up? We could do so for many reasons including the lack of good mentorship or availability of resources. Obstacles to mastery could also include **physical obstacles** (genetic limitations like height if you are trying to get better at playing basketball, for example), **technical obstacles** (difficulty in measuring progress or access to the right equipment or training material) or even **environmental obstacles** (like market forces, or difficulty in finding a good mentor).

Or we simply give up because it is too hard.

Emotional obstacles include the lack of belief, commitment, motivation or optimism. As behavioural science expert James Clear[5] puts it – there is a constant fight between the present

---

5   https://www.entrepreneur.com/article/248232; Last Accessed on 18 May 2016

you and the future you. It is natural human tendency to focus on what is just around the corner or what is at the end of your nose as opposed to what may happen years or decades from now.

THE DOUBLE WHAMMY OF INCOMPETENCE[6]

People who don't seem good at their jobs aren't necessarily aware of it. In some people, the parts of the brain involved with the proficiency of a task are also the parts of the brain which handle awareness of proficiency. In these cases, not only do these people not know, but they do not know that they do not know. This is called the Double Whammy of Incompetence.

This is also called the 'colleague from hell'.

So far into the future, we simply can't see the payoff. Present you wants instant returns and feels the future belongs to, well, the future. But future you wants you to invest time and effort so that you can benefit. How do you ensure that future you wins?

Visualization works beautifully to bring the benefits of the future you into the present,[7] and therefore enables you to feel better placed about investing in mastering something. Say, for example, your goal is to be sent by your company on a two-year project abroad, but you need to clear a particular exam and master some skill sets before you can be deputed, a process which may take a year or even two. Through visualization, you

---

6   http://news.harvard.edu/gazette/story/2010/04/building-a-better-brain/; Last Accessed on 18 May 2016

7   Ibid

can picture yourself enjoying the fruits of your labour two years hence. You can visualize getting that email from HR announcing your deputation, your boss's happy smile – or grunt, if they are not a smiler – and you can even picture calling your family and telling them that you have finally done it. Picture the phone call in minute detail. What would you say? What would their reaction be?

Another way to combat the urge to stay stuck where you are could be to penalize yourself if you don't follow through by putting a cost to your procrastination, either via money or in kind.[8] You could either tell yourself that for every time you skip a training session, for example, you will skip a night out with your friends. Or if you have five kilos to lose, you could declare your intent on social media, the trigger being public humiliation if you don't reach your goal. Whatever you do, attempt to rid yourself of things that distract you and be in spaces that help you make better decisions.[9] Robert Greene, in his book *Mastery*, also talks about resistance practice[10] where you need to go *against* all your natural instincts when you practise and simply power through.

WHEN YOU HIT A ROADBLOCK

- Visualize the results of what you want to master; it makes you that much more motivated when you are stuck.

---

8   Ibid
9   Ibid
10 Robert Greene, *Mastery*, London: Profile, 2012

- Don't let the best be the enemy of the good. Don't aim for perfection. You may never get the ideal situation or the perfect result. Do it and do it now. Done is better than perfect.
- Sometimes we procrastinate because a task seems too big to overcome. Reduce how intimidating it is by breaking it down into smaller mini-tasks.
- Establish deadlines. It brings clarity to a project and to your direction.

But sometimes, maybe the reason you are not seeing a payoff is because there isn't one. What if the area you've chosen to dominate has not been correctly selected? There is no point, for example, of being the God of Irrelevant Things. Or there is no point in mastering a skill that may soon become obsolete. What you need to master is, in itself, a monumentally important and strategic decision.

In the end, though, the important thing to understand is that there are people out there who know more than you do in your field; there will always be such people. Their proficiency is not so much because it is inherent, but because they have done their time in the trenches and learnt from their experiences.[11] Always be a learner, no matter how much you think you have already learnt. As Greene says, *'By valuing learning above all else, you will set the stage for creative expansion and the money will soon come to you.'*[12] Keep your long-term goal on your radar, keeping in mind

---

11 Ibid
12 Ibid

that mastery is not something unreachable, impossible or mystical. But it is, quite simply, a process.

The Bare Bones

LIFE LESSONS

From this chapter, you now know that

- Mastery is vital to the growth of a stupendous career.

- To achieve mastery, you need deliberate practice; according to estimates, it takes 10,000 hours of deliberate practice to achieve mastery over something.

- If you don't even try, how will you know what you can master?

- Mastery has professional, financial and prestige implications.

- The right mentor is the key to mastery. A bad teacher can set you back by years.

- You have to work very hard to master something. There is a reason it is called the pursuit of mastery: you have to chase it, it won't chase you.

- The obstacles to mastery include:

    o **Physical**: Where there may be physical difficulties that you may experience to achieve mastery.

    o **Emotional**: Where you may feel demotivated or psychologically unwilling to invest in mastery.

- o **Environmental**: Where the environment may not support mastery.
- o **Technical**: Lack of equipment.
- Visualization can beautifully help you master something.
- What you need to master is, in itself, a monumentally important and strategic decision.
- Mastery is not out of reach or impossible; it is, quite simply, a process.

WHAT DO YOU DO NOW?

4 **Identify a mentor who will help you attain mastery.** Can you identify a coach or a mentor who you think can help you achieve mastery over what you want to excel in? But when doing so, identify someone who has the time to pay attention to you, who has the knack for imparting knowledge and someone who is genuinely invested in your progress. Remember: how good your coach is could sometimes be how good *you get*.

CHAPTER SIX

Choosing to Choose
UNDERSTANDING DECISION-MAKING

In medicine, the decisions doctors make can be – quite literally – the difference between life and death. When a patient comes in with multiple – and sometimes contradictory – symptoms, even mistakes as deceptively simple as waiting and watching could lead to ignoring the underlying disease, leaving it to fester, prevail and sometimes even kill. How do you then, as a doctor, make the right decisions when you are presented with diseases whose symptoms fake right, but as soon as you get distracted, come in pounding from the left, smashing all your preconceived notions? It is no exaggeration to say that diseases can sometimes present themselves as dangerous wolves hidden in sheep's clothing.

But with age and experience, doctors become better at what they do and are able to spot the wolves hiding as the most innocent-looking sheep. But sometimes they still get foxed. They are so blinded by what things are *supposed* to be that they don't see things as they actually are. They see the same cases time and again and become so confident with a particular diagnosis that they fail to see that genuine biases – or thinking errors – have crept into their decision-making, sometimes with unspeakable, fatal consequences. And all of us, doctors or not, are guilty. At its very core, decision-making errors are very human ones.

Eighteen years ago, my mother complained of a pain in the abdomen. The usual medicines were not helping and the problem persisted. Then in her sixties, we decided to get her a USG ultrasound. I suppose that is the advantage of being in a family of doctors; we quickly get right to the jugular. The ultrasound indicated something out of the ordinary. Her common bile duct (CBD) – the organ responsible for transporting bile from the gall bladder to the small intestine – was showing signs of dilatation or enlargement. The sonologist guiding the ultrasound pointed it out and told me something I knew theoretically: CBD enlargement is one of the symptoms of cancer in the organ. And when I looked at it – standing there next to my mother – it *was* enlarged. I could see it. My heart sank.

Cancer of the CBD is one of the hardest to operate on and surgeons speak of it in tones of respect. Its particular location at the head of the pancreas means that it is complicated to remove surgically. But apprehensions aside, we had no choice it seemed; what started out as the road to a seemingly simple diagnosis sharply swerved on to the path of cancer. The medical investigation turned into a hunt for malignancy.

As it turned out, this was not the end but the start: of decision-making errors, of medical mistakes, of a falling domino of biases. But to continue, an endoscopy was done, the cells were extracted and sent to the pathology lab for cytology. The results came back and they confirmed what the gastroenterologist suspected.

Cancer. The cells looked cancerous.

According to the reports, a cytological examination of the cells – different from a biopsy, in which the cells are examined but not the tissue; cytology is also used to detect cancer – revealed that my mother had a suspicion of cancer of the CBD. The pathologist agreed with the gastroenterologist. It didn't help that my uncle, my mother's brother, was also operated on for the same reason: cancer of the CBD.

He died a few days after being in the ICU.

When a diagnosis like this comes in, you operate even on the basis of suspicion. This is because cancer of the CBD is tricky and could be fast-growing; most surgical teams would rather operate in haste and review at leisure. We started talking to surgeons. A new empathy for my own patients emerged. As a surgeon, it is all right to take a step back, be clinical and dispassionate when it is a patient, when it is someone you have met a few times. But what if it is your mother? What do you do then? The fact that her brother had been operated on under identical circumstances clearly sealed the deal. And the diagnosis? It ran in the family. *It is genetic,* we thought.

The surgery track started. Options were discussed. Dinner table conversations about the everyday were replaced with discussions of the surgical routes, techniques, the whens, the wheres and the hows. We began to meet surgical teams to discuss the best way to remove the tumour. We were talking in terms of morbidity and mortality, i.e., which techniques would limit the chance of her dying and which would increase it. My mother, an avid reader, preferred to watch television instead. She drowned us out, not wanting to get involved in the process of treatment. Her conversations reduced to speaking when being spoken to.

But for me, something didn't quite add up. The report was a suspicion and not a confirmation. The cells looked abnormal, but does abnormality always indicate cancer? Even though a vast number of cases meant that suspicious cells in this area *meant* cancer, what if this was the one case where it didn't? Also, the surgical risks of operating on a patient in her sixties was not to be discounted. Before scheduling the surgery, we decided to seek a second opinion. The case was presented to a medical oncologist. 'The cells are atypical,' he said. 'It is definitely suspicious but they may not be malignant. I don't think she has cancer.'

'All your mother has,' he continued, 'is an enlarged common bile duct. It is a genetic anomaly. It can run in families. That's why her brother had it.'

'She may not have cancer? But what about the report?'

'Get the pathology slides checked again,' replied the doctor.

The slides were reviewed by another pathologist.

It reported benign. Non-cancerous.

My mother did not have cancer. All she had was an enlarged CBD. Rare, but possible. But she did not have cancer.

How did this happen? What would have happened if we hadn't sought a second opinion?

Let's try and understand what led to the incorrect diagnosis. This entire process, from the investigation to the final diagnosis, was fraught with decision-making biases. The first was the **anchoring bias.** An anchoring bias is when the decision is influenced by the very *first* piece of information. A dilatated/enlarged CBD was the first thing the gastroenterologist looked at. Because enlarged CBDs are overwhelmingly associated with cancer, the gastroenterologist stopped looking for other possible reasons for the enlargement, relying too heavily on the initial information of a dilatated CBD. He next fell victim to the **confirmation bias**, where he started looking for evidence to confirm his belief, and not contradict it.

The cells were collected from the CBD because the gastroenterologist was so sure it was cancer, falling prey to the **overconfidence bias**; he was so sure of his diagnosis. This bias carried to the next doctor, the pathologist, who was influenced by the first piece of information, too. When the cells were studied during the biopsy process, they *looked suspicious.* And *could* mean cancer. The pathologist *thought* they looked cancerous because **the gastroenterologist was suspicious**. There was a fifty-fifty chance that it was not. But she went with the cancer diagnosis because that is what it could *mean in this context, influenced by the initial diagnosis.* She was also aware of the reputation of the doctor who had referred her to me. He was rarely wrong. She was subconsciously influenced by his excellence and expertise; she also fell prey to the **authority bias**. The doctor referring the case influenced the decision as much as what she was seeing before her. If he suspected it, looking at the evidence, he must be right, she may have thought.

Four biases have already skewed the case.

Do you see what happened here? When the time came to review the cells, when the decision could have swung either way, the pathologist went with the prevailing *belief* – not the prevailing *knowledge* – and made the diagnosis. Then, based on the pathology report and the ultrasound, the group of surgeons that were discussing the surgery fell prey to the fifth bias, the **group think bias**, described in the *Harvard Business Review* as striving 'for consensus at the cost of a realistic appraisal of alternative courses of action'.[1] In other words, when the surgeons were discussing the case, it was more important to **agree** than to question. By discussing surgical techniques that would enhance or limit her chances of survival, the sixth bias came into play, the **controllability bias**: decisions were made on the misleading belief that the outcome could be controlled by the surgeons, increasing the risk of performing risky procedures. It didn't help that my uncle died under extremely similar circumstances which was also a part of forming the **recency** or **availability bias**. This would mean that the doctors were **influenced** by recent events within the family while making the diagnosis. Seven biases in all.

During all this, my mother's abdominal pain receded. It was simply a bad case of gastritis. The doctor who we went to for a second opinion asked us to keep a watch just in case any other symptoms popped up.

It has been about eighteen years.

We are still keeping a watch.

As it turns out, her brother, my uncle, *was* misdiagnosed and the doctors fell prey to the biases.

But he was not as lucky.

Decision-making biases eventually killed him.

---

1 John Beshears, and Francesca Gino, 'Leaders as Decision Architects', *Harvard Business Review*, May 2015

If only we knew then what we know now.

How the Brain Makes Decisions

There is a science to the way we make decisions, a pattern that the brain follows when decisions are being made. We all have a decision-making centre in the brain located in the ventromedial aspect of the prefrontal cortex in the frontal lobe – just behind the eye sockets. While most of the decisions we make will not kill us – unless of course we're feeling particularly suicidal – they will, most certainly, have the ability to harm our careers or our lives. The question then is – how do we choose to choose?

How the brain makes decisions is a bit like a three-person relay race. The decision-making centre in the prefrontal cortex sends out a message to the site where dopamine is produced in the brain. Dopamine is a chemical or molecule present in our bodies that helps us decide between alternatives.[2] This, in turn, sends a message to the striatum, which then sends the message back to the prefrontal cortex. In this never-ending game of message relay – this happens in a matter of milliseconds or fewer – we decide to get out of bed, brush our teeth, check our phones as soon as we wake up and maybe smile at our neighbour on our way to work. When we repeat this enough times, it becomes a habit.

In the body, there is a fatty substance called myelin which covers nerve fibres and has the function of increasing the speed of electrical communication between the neurons.[3] The thicker

---

2   Jonah Lehrer, *The Decisive Moment: How the Brain Makes up Its Mind*, Edinburgh: Canongate, 2009

3   http://www.brainfacts.org/brain-basics/neuroanatomy/ articles/2015/myelin/; Last Accessed on 18 May 2016

the myelination, the more mature the person; the greater the intelligence, the better the ability to see the long-term effects of the decision being made and consequently, the better the decision-making. That is why teenagers don't always make good long-term decisions, and why it is so hard for parents to get through to them. Their brains, by and large, are not myelinated yet. They cannot see themselves in the future and find it hard to relate to the consequences of their actions. Myelination occurs usually at the age of about twenty-two to twenty-four years on an average.

Interestingly, the brain is also wired to make decisions. The brain *likes* to make decisions because it likes to complete loops. It doesn't like questions hanging in the air and wants closure. This is called the Zeigarnik effect, named after a Lithuanian psychologist Bluma Zeigarnik who concluded in her doctoral thesis that **the human brain likes to finish tasks.** She first noticed this phenomenon when observing waiters. She observed that they took complicated food orders and once they delivered them, they forgot them. But she noticed that incomplete orders remained in waiters' minds until they completed them.[4] Intrigued, she started replicating this conclusion by asking subjects to solve various puzzles and then interrupting them while they were doing it. People recalled all the incomplete tasks 90 per cent better than the tasks they had completed, children even more so. This means that the brain continues to remember incomplete tasks until they are completed, until the loop is closed. Quite simply, Close your loops.

Decision-making is linked to the completing of loops. When

---

4 http://blog.sandglaz.com/zeigarnik-effect-scientific-key-to-better-work/; Last Accessed on 18 May 2016

you can't complete an action, the thought lingers. And the more things you have pending, the harder it is for you to do other new things. Take a moment right now to think about the things that are pending in your life: an unreturned phone call or an unexpressed apology or an unpaid dry-cleaning bill; there would probably be many things lingering on in your mind. You think about it then you leave it alone and go on to do other things. But the brain never forgets and it all piles up, slowly crowding your mind, pulling you down. In the chapter on 'Understanding Willpower', we ask you to identify your nuisance tumours in order to alert you to the fact that seemingly innocent unfinished tasks may, in fact, not be so innocent after all.

The brain is also not good at multi-tasking. The one-body, many-hands approach may not always actually work for you. When you decide to do too many things at once – too many New Year resolutions, for example – your brain gets overwhelmed and instead of fulfilling one thing perfectly, you end up not doing anything at all. This is because you may be attempting to change too many habits and you only have a limited stock of willpower and because, as studies suggest, the human brain is programmed to do only one thing excellently at a time. In the chapter 'Understanding Willpower', I will get into this in greater detail but for now, when it comes to any major changes or decisions, scientists advise you to focus on one thing at a time.

But while your brain loves making decisions, it can also let you down and sabotage the decisions you make. Remember that great tug-of-war that we addressed in 'The Science of Change'? The part of the brain that loves change, the frontal lobe, is constantly being pulled back by the part of the brain that hates change, the amygdala. The same applies to the decision-making process. Routine is one of the biggest saboteurs of decision-making. The amygdala – the part of your brain which has a strong craving for routine and a desire for habits – pulls you back into your comfort zone and can push you to make those decisions that are regular and comfortable. Simply put, the brain likes to make decisions as much as it likes to feel comfortable. This is one of the reasons doctors get trapped in a narrow frame and start looking at diagnoses that they have traditionally been familiar with, sometimes becoming blind to their choices.

And the next time you can't walk past a bakery without stepping in and buying yourself a rich, creamy pastry, blame your brain. There is also a chemical in the brain that makes you prone to impulse. Mono amine oxidase (MAO) is the chemical that controls impulse. Some have less MAO, some have more. Walter Mischel created one of the most important and famous social experiments in psychology: the 'Marshmallow Test'. It was to find out if *people with more self-control go on to lead more successful lives.* In this test, children were offered marshmallows on the condition that if they wanted it immediately, they would get one but if they waited for fifteen minutes, they would get two. While we will understand this in more detail later in the book, the answer to the question posed by Walter Mischel is 'yes'. The more self-control you practise, the more successful you become.

Types of Decisions

But if we understand the brain and its decision-making abilities, how do we work on making better decisions? We could, for example, learn from understanding the concept of delaying gratification when, for example, at an interview, we are offered the chance to make more money at a job we know is not right for us, waiting instead for the right opportunity. It also helps us be more conscious of our behaviour and change it, if need be.

We could also understand the different ways our brain makes decisions and can decide when and how to employ which process. Daniel Kahneman, in his book *Thinking, Fast and Slow*, outlined two sets of decision-making processes or systems that we employ, whether we are aware of it or not. Some decisions we make are knee-jerk and instinctive while others are made patiently, over time, with deliberation and after doing our homework.

You are at the airport; your boss had called asking you to take an earlier flight to make a late-evening meeting back at the office. You are standing in line waiting to talk to the airline staff at the ticket window to make the change but it is a long line. *Why can't they open up another window,* you think, as you fan yourself with a copy of your flight details. Suddenly, your wishes are answered. Another window opens up, almost by magic. Instinctively, you find yourself rushing to this new window, elbowing anyone who tries to beat you to it. You don't know how you got there. All you know is that 'something' propelled you to get there, and to get there *first.* Daniel Kahneman would call this certain something **System One** decision-making – an 'automatic, instinctive, emotional'[5] process of making decisions that are so quick and

---

5   Daniel Kahneman, *Thinking, Fast and Slow,* London: Penguin Books, 2012

seamless that you don't know how you arrived at them. All you know is that you are now at the new ticket window.

System One is the kind of decision-making that is done on a 'gut' or instinctive level and especially refers to decisions that need to be made in minutes or in a matter of hours or in emergency situations. But there seems to be something about the word 'gut' which seems mysterious or inexplicable. For example, whenever I hear the word 'gut', it seems to relate to decisions that cannot be explained or are somehow linked to evolutionary or primal instincts.

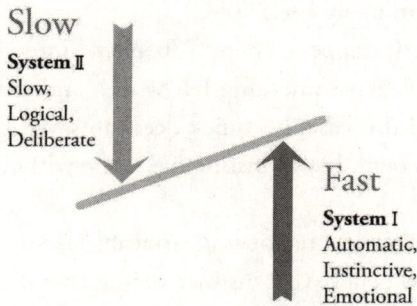

Slow

System II
Slow,
Logical,
Deliberate

Fast

System I
Automatic,
Instinctive,
Emotional

Two Kinds of Thinking: Daniel Kahneman

A parent throwing out their arm to protect their child if they brake too hard at a traffic light could be likened, for example, to a parental instinct, something as old as human evolution. A gut reaction, they would probably later say, when they would recount the episode to family and friends. Another example could be when you are meeting a person for the first time, whether you like or dislike them is also a gut feeling and you don't exactly know what led you to that decision.

But is the gut always as mysterious and nebulous as that? It is impossible not to understand gut decisions without the story of a team of firemen who put out a fire in an apartment block in the United States. The fire chief and his band of men were later looking for the source of the fire when the chief suddenly had the uncomfortable feeling that something was very wrong. He immediately started to evacuate the team, following them out himself. Within seconds of them exiting the building, the floor that they were standing on gave way. If they had remained, they would have probably been killed.

What exactly happened here? When later interviewed, the fire chief just said that something felt wrong and that he just had to get out. In this case, his quick decision saved the lives of his team and his own. It was instinctive, done without thinking.

Or was it?

Snap judgements are not as inexplicable as was once thought. Scientists now believe that instinctive judgements stem from the brain recognizing a previous pattern based on the experiences you have had in the past. Decisions are made at lightning speeds because the context is familiar. In other words, it is 'instinctive' because it was a decision that didn't need deliberation or time by your brain. It is not gut – a more mysterious concept – but just the speed that *makes it seem instinctive.* But in fact it is subject to the same biases and thinking. That is why gut feelings pay off sometimes, but not all the time.

Scientists recommend that you trust a snap decision or use your gut to make decisions only when you have *experience* in that area. Should you trust your gut on the first day of your new job? If you haven't been exposed to the situation or environment before, probably not. Should you take a punt on a new supplier in your new business? If you are new to the industry, probably not. The gut is something that *can* be questioned.

System Two[6] thinking, on the other hand, is what Kahneman has described as slow, logical and deliberate. Here is when you employ due diligence, when you take your time, when you weigh your options and then slowly and carefully make your decisions. This is what I have to do all the time, even with my more routine cases. Let us take, for example, the case of a forty-five-year-old woman with an eight centimetre fibroid, presenting symptoms like heavy menstrual cycles and weakness. Even for a seemingly common case like this, the approach has to be systematic and logical. Does the patient need an ultrasound only or an MRI as well? Is there a need to do a complete body profile? Would removal of the fibroid be enough or should a hysterectomy be performed? Does she need the procedure now or can she wait for six months? Is there an alternative to surgery? Is there a possibility that her tumour may be malignant? Even in these fairly simple cases, complex decisions are involved because in medicine there is no such thing as two perfectly identical cases.

Behavioural scientists have zeroed in on the two main ways of making most System Two decisions: either it is a quest for the perfect solution or one that is simply good enough. In other words, people are categorized into whether they have a

---

6   Daniel Kahneman, *Thinking, Fast and Slow*, London: Penguin Books, 2012

maximizing or satisficing approach towards making decisions. **Maximizers**[7] look at wanting the best possible solution – no inferior option will be considered – and they carefully weigh every option possible before making a decision. **Satisficers** – a combination of the words satisfy and suffice[8] – know that the best may not always be available, and while they also have high standards, they settle for what is good enough.

Dr Barry Schwartz, a psychology professor at Swarthmore College, Pennsylvania, researched 548 college students who were about to graduate and were looking for a job. The findings of the 2006 study – which were published in the journal Psychological Sciences – revealed that being picky helped. Maximizers got better paying jobs and their salaries were on an average 20 per cent higher that their more satisficing counterparts. But that was not the more interesting aspect of the study. Surprisingly, even though the maximizers succeeded in getting more money, they were *not* as happy as the satisficer group because they always felt that the final option wasn't good enough.

While they may eventually get the best, maximizers also run the risk of making decisions which never really satisfy them. Satisficers, as the name suggests, are happier with their eventual choices. They already know that they may be bypassing better options, but are okay to not explore them. Satisficers also move

---

7   Barry Schwartz, *The Paradox of Choice*, New York: Harper Perennial, 2013

8   http://www.wsj.com/articles/how-you-make-decisions-says-a-lot-about-how-happy-you-are-1412614997; Last Accessed on 18 May 2016

faster because they don't agonize over choices while maximizers run the risk of never making a decision at all. I once had a surgeon friend of mine who wanted to buy a laparoscopic camera ten to fifteen years ago. When I bought mine, he said he would wait to buy his, claiming that he would buy it based on my experience with it. The next time I saw him, I had already upgraded to the next camera and he repeated what he said, that he'd wait for my review on this new camera before buying his. This continued and while I'm now on my seventh camera, he still hasn't bought his; all because nothing was good enough. In laparoscopic surgery, your equipment is key to building your career. The inaction must have cost him both financially and professionally.

Most people practise *both* forms of decision-making, depending on the decision's relative importance to their life; some people maximize in decisions like finding a life partner and satisfice when deciding on selecting a name for their baby. Do note that, according to the study, there is no evidence to suggest that either type are more prone to making bad decisions. Satisficers also have high standards but perhaps not as high as maximizers. As Dr Schwartz concludes, 'Maximizers make good decisions and end up feeling bad about them. Satisficers make good decisions and end up feeling good.'[9] Theoretically, you shouldn't settle until you are really happy with something, but sometimes accepting a good

9   http://www.wsj.com/articles/how-you-make-decisions-says-a-lot-about-how-happy-you-are-1412614997; Last Accessed on 18 May 2016

enough option enables you to move along. Whatever you decide, it is important to make peace with it and move on. Even if you get it wrong, it is not the end of the world.

Decision-Making Biases

Whether it's System One or System Two, maximizer of satisficer, you can't avoid decision-making biases. A team that included a gastroenterologist, pathologists, sonologists and surgeons could not avoid the domino of errors that had crept into my mother's case. And if my uncle died when he should have lived, what does this say about the way decisions are influenced? According to the *Harvard Business Review*, the two main causes of bad decisions are insufficient motivation and cognitive or thinking biases. While motivation or volition is what we will be covering in 'Volition: The Anatomy of the Want', it is important to understand the kind of cognitive or thinking biases we get trapped in. Tick the box if you've found yourself in this situation[10] (answers on page 103):

1. You are in charge of your company's offsite this year. You have decided that you would rather go with a hotel on the beach because the pictures looked nice online and you have warmed to the idea. You spend time looking for reviews and online recommendations that support your decision. ☐

---

10 John Beshears and Francesca Gino, 'Leaders as Decision Architects', *Harvard Business Review*, May, 2015

2. Your boss has informed you that sales have plummeted because of an inefficient supply chain system. You immediately start researching this conclusion further. ☐

3. You have been called for a group brainstorming session and by the end of it, you realize that you have started to side with what is popular, even though it is not *exactly* what you would see as a way forward. You think it is better to agree than to disagree. After all, it is hard to get everyone to agree, right? ☐

4. You are so concerned about how to *not* make losses on a project that you start investigating ways to reduce that risk. ☐

5. You continue to operate a loss-making business unit because you have already made considerable investments in it in the hope that it will turn the corner. ☐

6. You pump in even more money and other resources into the loss-making business unit despite evidence that it won't become profitable because you have already invested so much in it already, in the hope that it will work out. ☐

7. You have in the past underestimated how dangerous the competition is and have made decisions without factoring in all the possible external threats. ☐

8. When you have made decisions in the past that haven't worked, you have realized in retrospect that you overestimated how much of the situation was in your control. ☐

9. 'If It Ain't Broke, Don't Fix It' is something you have found yourself saying on more than one occasion when faced with a work problem that you felt was better left alone.   ☐

10. Many times in your career you have made decisions about your team or a project keeping short-term objectives in mind.   ☐

11. Your department head wants you to launch a micro-site on your company website. You use the web designer recommended by a colleague from another team because they had a great experience working with her.   ☐

12. You have found yourself replicating – with minor adjustments – the award-winning solution you designed for a client when pitching for business for those from the same industry. It is more efficient, right?   ☐

If you have ticked:

1. You could have fallen prey to the **confirmation bias.** This is when you start to look for things that support your belief rather than contradict it, and you are partial in your search for evidence.

2. Your boss has focused your attention in the direction of the supply chain as a reason for poor sales. But could the reason be rooted elsewhere? While nobody wants to be the one who tells the emperor he has no clothes, making decisions based on the first piece of information received is called the **anchoring bias.** This particular example could also be an **authority bias** because you are processing the information without question as it is coming in from your boss. If your boss says it, it must be true, right?

3. You have just ticked off what could be a **group think bias** where it is more important to agree than actually evaluate the problem in a more realistic or objective way.

4. That could be a **loss aversion bias** where your focus and energy is directed towards avoiding making losses as opposed to looking for information and taking steps that would direct you towards making a profit, thereby making you more risk averse than usual.

5. You could have just made a decision influenced by a **sunk-cost bias or sunk-cost fallacy.** The fact that you have already invested in something interferes with your ability to be objective.

6. You may have just fallen prey to the **escalation-of-commitment bias** where you are influenced by an earlier decision to throw more money and resources at a possible loss-making situation.

7. That could have just been the **overconfidence bias** kicking in.

8. You may have been blinkered by the **controllability bias** which leads you to believe that you have more control over the outcome.

9. This could just be the **status quo bias** where you are comfortable with the way things currently are, especially when there is no pressure to change things.

10. Think back to understand if you may have been influenced by the **present bias** which doesn't look at the long-term impact of things.

11. Believe it or not, even something as innocuous as a word-of-mouth recommendation could be a **recency** or **availability bias,** when your decision is influenced by recent events, like a recent success or failure.

12. While there is nothing uncommon with this, even this potentially harmless practice may mean that you have been influenced by an **outcome bias,** in that your decision may have been influenced by the fact that it worked for you in the past. The question is, is it a good decision only when the outcome is good?

Many people confuse the process of decision-making with the *outcome*. While it seems counter-intuitive, decisions are actually about processes, not results. If you have made a decision that had a good outcome, it does *not* automatically make it a good decision. The result could have been favourable because you were just lucky. Similarly, during a complicated surgery, if the patient died but the doctor did all the right things, does it mean he or she made bad decisions because the patient eventually died? When making decisions, even past outcomes can sometimes be misleading.

Decision-Making Environments

The Power of a Question

You are at your favourite restaurant. You have flipped through the menu and are placing your order, a chicken club sandwich, with your waiter. After noting it down, he then asks you if you want French fries or potato wedges with it. You think for a second. 'Fries,' you say. Sounds like a regular transaction, right? Wrong. The waiter offered you two options. And that is the key word here – *Offered*. The decision-making environment – in this case, a harmless enough question from the waiter – presented you with the feeling that you only had two options to choose from. When, in fact, you could have created a third option for yourself: no potatoes at all. Life, work, personal relationships may always present you with a 'this' or 'that' option. You must examine the options presented to you and ask yourself whether you can actually choose secret options three and four, which could be 'both' or 'none'. It is amazing what power a simple question has. And how it influences your decision-making.

Another famous example is the one set by Stephen R. Covey in his book *The 8th Habit: From Effectiveness to Greatness*. He poses a question: if you had to go in for surgery and had to choose between a surgeon who was honest but incompetent and a surgeon who was competent but dishonest, who would you choose? It is an interesting question because allowing an incompetent surgeon to operate on you could have fatal consequences while a dishonest but skilled surgeon would operate on you even if there wasn't any need to operate on you in the first place. The best answer, Covey concludes, is to go to the honest surgeon for confirming the need to operate and the skilled one for the actual surgery. *Why choose one or the other when you can have both?*

You can design your own decision-making environment by offering options to your team, your seniors, your clients and your vendors. Give people options to choose from; certain tangible actionables that would enable you all to move forward. For example, you can even use this to *prevent* someone from making a decision. Say a team member wants to leave for another team because, as she has articulated, she feels there are limited opportunities for creative development. How do you prevent her from going from A to B? The only way you can do that is to give her C, which is a more *attractive* option.[11] Do keep in mind that it is hard to demotivate someone who has made up her mind of going to B, the next attractive option. You have to give her a better option, which is C. This also works for talking yourself out of something.

---

11 Edward De Bono, *Lateral Thinking*, London: Penguin, 2010

Also, as discussed in 'The Science of Change', the fewer options you give or have, the faster the decision-making process. Barry Schwartz, in his book *The Paradox of Choice: Why More Is Less,* says that while an absence of choice is a dismal thing, an overload of choice could contribute to anxiety, stress and unsatisfactory decisions; in some cases, even clinical depression. Reduce the options to reduce the anxiety.

But that is easier said than done. Because of the immense power of the media and the prevalence of technology, you are being coaxed and manipulated into making decisions. When you order a book online, why is it that the next time you search for a book, the website presents you with similar options as a first line of selection? Artificial intelligence, intelligent placement and various other techniques are being used to persuade you to make decisions that you may not have ordinarily made. Be vigilant about decision-making triggers around you.

There also comes a time when your brain gets tired of making decisions. Decision fatigue is a very real situation. If you are going into surgery, for example, here is a tip: schedule your operation as early as possible in the morning because that is when the surgeon is the freshest in the day. By the end of the surgeon's operating schedule, he or she has made so many surgical decisions that they are more prone to biases or errors.

No matter what you decide, it is important to cultivate an environment that does not fear failure. The fear of failure itself could be a monumental hurdle that could lead people to simply never move out of their comfort zones or repeat the same mistakes over and over again. You have to move ahead and see what happens.

Keep in mind, even taking no decision is a decision after all.

What If You Are Stuck?

Uncorking Bottlenecks

If you are stuck making all-important decisions, why not try a few of these bottle-openers?

1. **Eliminate Options:** Given that the brain makes the best decisions when it comes to choosing between two options, narrow down the options from a wide range to just two. You can do this by eliminating the least desirable option, reviewing what is left and then again eliminating the least desirable option from the new set, and so on until you reach the final two.

2. **Find a Trench-mate:** Look for someone who, in your opinion, has been in the same hole as you have and has managed to make good decisions. Since they have also been in the unique position you are in and only they can truly understand your dilemma, their advice could prove invaluable.

3. **Be an Outsider:** When it comes to making decisions, act like an outsider. Pretend as if it is not your decision to make but someone else's. Be your own devil's advocate and try to poke holes in your own arguments or the arguments of others.

4. **Test your Assumption:** If it is possible, use a smaller sample to actually test and see if your theory is right.

Ask questions, take an opinion poll, even hunt for objective and constructive feedback.

5. **Reduce Personal Biases:** When making a decision, ask yourself if you are choosing a particular option because you like it or because it is genuinely the right thing to do. What if the least favourite option was actually the **best** one? I ask this, for example, to patients who want to avoid surgery because it is their least favourite option, even though it may be the best one for them.

6. **Zoom In, Zoom Out:** In laparoscopic surgery, as cameras are used to perform minimally invasive surgeries, surgeons not only have to zoom in to the problem area, but also need to zoom out to ensure that no vital organs were being affected during the surgery, thereby operating in the context of the problem. Look at the big picture. Instead of zooming in to a narrow field, zoom out to understand the decision in a wider context. Would it matter if this decision was incorrect after five, ten or even twenty years?

7. **Understand the Payoff:** Understand that material gains like cars, houses, bonuses and lottery winnings provide short-term happiness. If these are your primary motivations, understand they may not give you the happiness you want.

8. **Try the Vanishing-Options Test:** When evaluating a line of treatment, I sometimes try the vanishing-options test. So I ask myself, what if the patient was in a remote town and the facilities for surgery were not available? Would I treat this patient differently or is surgery the only option? Even as a surgeon, I don't recommend it until I am certain that the patient has no option. The vanishing-options test helps me with trickier cases to ensure that I don't succumb to my own biases by selecting an option within my specialty and comfort zone.

9. **The Black Swan:** Look for the Black Swan. For centuries, and not just decades, it was thought that swans were white. But since the spotting of a black swan in Australia in 1697 by Williem de Vlamingh, it has become a symbol of the improbable, the impossible. Think about outcomes that you believed might have been impossible and apply it to your situation. Sometimes, real life is stranger than fiction. What could be a black swan in your profession or business?

STRATEGIC INTUITION

When Archimedes was trying to figure out the problem of weighing extremely huge objects that could not be physically weighed – like ships – he eventually found his answer in a bathtub. A term coined by William Duggen,[12] **strategic intuition** has been defined as a sudden insight – an 'Aha' moment – into a problem that has been bothering you for a while. After mulling over the problem for days or weeks on end, you suddenly get the answer when you weren't thinking about it, like during a movie or when you wake up first thing in the morning. The brain works in very interesting ways.

In On War, Carl Von Clausewitz has further elaborated on strategic intuition as **pattern recognition**, i.e., when you feed your brain with the problem and it matches with past experiences buried in your brain.[13] When you feed a problem into your brain, your brain works furiously behind the scenes to find you a solution. It runs through your past experiences that have been stored in the deeper recesses of your brain and matches the appropriate ones to the problem at hand. And when it makes the right connection or match, the flash of insight is what

---

12 Williem R. Duggan, *Strategic Intuition: The Creative Spark in Human Achievement*, Columbia Business School Publishing, New York: Columbia University Press, 2007

13 Carl von, Clausewitz, *On War*, Charleston, South Carolina: Createspace, 2013

makes the lightbulb in your head go off, even when you weren't paying attention to the problem. Intuition has been defined as a process that is both unconscious and associative because you are not aware of the rapid work your brain is doing to find a solution to your problem.

Can strategic intuition be learnt? Yes, if you do one of the simplest things and free your mind of past failures or biases. Since the essentials of strategic intuition are pattern recognition, with pattern matching based on past experiences, it is crucial to let your brain 'match' your problem with the 'answer' based on your past experience of the problem. The reason this works so well is because not only does the brain like to complete loops, it likes to solve problems. In other words, your brain is always, always at your service. Trust your brain. It'll know what to do.

DOPAMINE[14]

Dopamine, according to Jonah Lehrer in *The Decisive Moment: How the Brain Makes Up its Mind*, is the is the 'common neural currency of the mind'. It is the molecule which enables us to choose between alternatives and is what brain cells use to communicate with each other. It is also what gives you that feeling of 'intuition'.

---

14 Jonah Lehrer, *The Decisive Moment: How The Brain Makes Up Its Mind*, Edinburgh: Cannongate, 2009

THE BARE BONES
LIFE LESSONS

From this chapter, you now know that

- Decision-making errors are essentially human ones.

- The human brain likes to make decisions. But not too many at a time. It is programmed to do only one thing excellently at one time.

- Routine is one of the biggest saboteurs of decision-making. The brain likes to make decisions as much as it likes to be comfortable.

- The more self-control you practise, the more successful you are.

- You can't always trust your gut. Make decisions with your gut only in areas you are experienced in.

- With trial and error, know which decisions work better with a maximizing approach or a satisficing one.

- Create your own decision-making environments. Exploit the power of a question.

What Do You Do Now?

5 **Be aware of how you make decisions.** What clouds your judgement? Emotions and biases can affect how we perceive the world around us and may affect our ability to make good decisions. Have biases crept into your thinking? Are you succumbing to an artificially-created decision-making environment? For example, we value advice that we have paid for and the decisions we make as a result of that advice are taken more seriously.

CHAPTER SEVEN

Learnings from Medical Risk Taking

Medicine is a never-ending quest for certainty: a certainty to know, to eradicate, to cure. It is an unquenchable mission to ensure that pain is permanently alleviated, life expectancy is extended and diseases are prevented. But while newer answers are being found to older questions, it still doesn't plug the stream of new questions that our bodies throw up; that is just the nature of the way both humans and disease seem to be evolving. Two patients with the same symptoms could have different reactions to medications, anaesthesia and treatment courses because of their make-up and their environment. In medicine, in relationships and in careers, nothing is certain and risks are taken all the time. But can lessons be learnt from the way doctors take risks? And what is the difference between risk and recklessness?

Christmas 2002: Neena walked into my room looking like she was almost nine months pregnant. I looked up, surprised. Maybe there was an extreme complication, I mentally shrugged, because most of my OB/GYN patients are usually taken care of by my team of capable doctors. She sat down gingerly, trying to hide her stomach – not uncommon for some patients. But as I started to ask her questions, I realized she wasn't pregnant.

It wasn't a baby. It was a fibroid.

A benign tumour in her uterus had grown to the point where she looked like she was carrying a child. Imagine how enormous this fibroid would look in comparison to the average fibroid which would be so small that you would just about be able to see it in an ultrasound. And considering that the uterus is smaller than the size of a tennis ball in most cases and weighs about 75 grams, imagine how much heavier this would be. It was something I had never seen before.

It was obvious that Neena's fibroid needed to be removed because of the health and cosmetic implications. For personal reasons, Neena was insistent that the surgery be performed laparoscopically and not by cutting open the abdomen. Laparoscopy is where science meets art. It is science because instead of one large cut that opens up the abdomen enabling the surgeon to see, for example, the fibroid(s) at a glance and just remove them, laparoscopy entails making smaller one-centimetre incisions *around* the abdominal cavity to provide access for telescopes with attached cameras to enter the body. Based on this visual perspective, the fibroid is then broken up into tiny pieces and taken out piece by piece. It is an art because the surgeon never actually sees the abdomen directly. Depth perception then becomes critical. The last thing any surgeon wants to do is damage healthy structures or organs by mistake.

And in this particular case, depth perception would be extremely hard. The sheer size of this tumour meant that I would be unable to see the uterus clearly since the fibroid had taken up the entire space and a number of complications could occur, including excessive bleeding. The medical reason for the bleeding is that the blood supply to the uterus and the fibroids comes from the uterine arteries. These arteries are attached to the fibroids – almost like an umbilical cord – and supply blood, enabling the tumour to grow. Given the size of the tumour, the uterine arteries, which are pulsating with blood, would be huge. And so would the blood loss when they would have to be cut to free the fibroid. But the patient's insistence, along with the belief that it could still be technically done, made me explore this as an option.

I did whatever research I could. I scanned articles and read numerous journals trying to track down a precedent. And all I could find was this: the maximum size of a fibroid that had been removed laparoscopically was ten centimetres in size. Neena's was double at almost twenty-one centimetres. No one else had removed a fibroid of this size laparoscopically. There was no medical precedent anywhere in the world.

I decided to go ahead anyway.

I knew that while there were calculated risks, I could go in and assess the situation and retract my steps, if need be. I didn't have to cut anything, touch anything. But I did anticipate blood loss. I also kept the option of doing conventional open surgery – with a large incision – if, for some reason, I could not do it laparoscopically.

In the first few minutes of the operation, my initial response was to stitch her back up, put down my instruments and get the hell out of there. The fibroid was *immense*, but I ploughed on. Slowly, over what seemed like an eternity but was actually about two hours, I managed to separate it from the arteries that were clinging on to it.

And that is when the bleeding started.

Furious, profuse, gushing, angry bleeding.

Suddenly there was blood everywhere. I couldn't see a thing. Surgeons hate bleeding because it adds more work to the case, adds time to the operation, interferes with the clarity of the view and can lead to mistakes. Uterus, bowel loops, nerves and more blood vessels can accidentally get cut when excessive bleeding cannot be controlled.

The other reason surgeons dislike excessive blood loss is that it is a reflection of their operative skills. In doctors' lounges, surgeons whisper about other surgeons who lose excessive amounts of blood during routine operations. It is never talked about openly, but these conversations float around as unchecked rumours in doctors' circles.

This patient was bleeding more than I liked.

'Can we transfuse some blood?' I asked my anaesthesiologist wife, Manju, who was now getting concerned.

I realized that if I quickly sutured both the uterine arteries, I could cut off the blood source of the fibroid. Doing so would limit the blood loss and enable easier extraction of the fibroid. And it began to work, but only to be faced with the next problem: extraction.

Given that you are operating using small incisions or 'keyholes', you can't remove a fibroid in its original form in laparoscopy. You have to cut it up into smaller pieces and then take it out. But how do you slice something the size of a football into something the size of a small strip? You do it patiently but as quickly as possible because the patient is under anaesthesia the whole time.

Using a surgical instrument called a morcellator which, as the name suggests, cuts tissue into smaller bits or morsels, I took two and a half hours to slice the biggest of all fibroids into tiny little pieces. This was turning out to be so time-consuming that I had to alternate between two morcellators because these instruments were battery-powered at the time and their batteries kept depleting.

I wanted to give up many, many times, but gradually, finally, unbelievably, it was done. The fibroid was weighed at the end of the surgery and at 3.47 kilograms, it turned out to be the largest fibroid ever to be removed laparoscopically in the world and went on to become a Guinness World Record.

A Guinness World Record. My life was never the same again.

Given the size of the tumour, the patient had a tumultuous post-operative recovery, but finally went home and recovered. Nine years later, in 2009, I removed the world's heaviest uterus laparoscopically. This was my second entry into the *Guinness Book of World Records*.

I now hold two records.

Taking calculated risks elevates careers. In the absence of a precedent, in the absence of existing validation, I went ahead and operated anyway and came out from the experiences with two record-breaking surgeries which changed the course of my medical practice. It was an extremely difficult decision to make and it could have not worked out as well. Even during regular low-risk surgical procedures, there are so many things that can go wrong like bleeding from cutting a large artery by mistake, or bowel, bladder or ureteric injury, infection and so on. The list can be endless, especially if you think too much about it.

Which is actually the point. Think, but think strategically. Take chances in your career and don't stop taking them. Because of my success at the first record-breaking surgery, I did the second. Successful risk taking begets more successful risk taking. Raise your hand during meetings, pitch in for projects that may be out of your comfort zone, write that book or take a year off and get a degree. The human brain *likes* taking risks; it is what makes it feel alive, it is what breathes that freshness into your work, your career. Without our inherent risk-taking ability we wouldn't have discovered air travel, penicillin, a cure for small pox, the Internet and cell phones. It is the simplest lesson you can learn. No risk, no reward.

In medicine, when the risk pays off, you can literally be giving someone a chance to live life anew. All professions have risks, all decisions have risks and all relationships have risks. And you have to take them. Because even though you *will* fail from time to time, you will never move upwards by being boxed in.

DEFENSIVE MEDICINE

Doctors are no strangers to risk reduction and many practise a form of medicine known as defensive medicine. It is a method of practising medicine that is more geared towards protecting physicians from lawsuits than always acting in the best interests of the patient. According to a survey in Pennsylvania in the United States, a whopping 93 per cent of doctors practise medicine defensively. Signs that your doctor may be on the defensive are if he or she:

1. Asks you to take more tests than you need.
2. Prescribes more meds than you need.
3. Refers you to doctors or other specialists even if you may not need it.
4. Suggest procedures that may be invasive, like biopsies, to confirm a diagnosis that is not likely to be the case.

Of course, you would know that the above is being done if you get a second opinion, or even if you directly ask your doctor if these processes are necessary. Doctors know that they are not liable if they over-investigate or ask you to take unnecessary tests. But that is not always in your best interests. One of the ways you can bypass this particular situation is to ask doctors what they would do if you were their relative or a close friend. **Ask doctors what they would do, not what they recommend.**

But how do you differ between risk and recklessness?

To answer that, I can give you another surgical example. Surgeons practise something called risk stratification, i.e., classifying patients or surgeries into high-risk and low-risk. We arrive at that conclusion by ordering tests, studying the case, reading up, taking out a detailed family history and then deciding whether surgery needs to take place. Surgery is usually the last option, even for those performing it. Because every surgery is a risk anyway, assessing the risk means understanding all the possible outcomes and taking the best decision, both in terms of the safety and interest of the patient, as well as in the best interests for your career. When I operate, I expose the patient to pain and other risks, so I have to be sure that when we decide to opt for surgery, there is no other course.

If you are taking risks, take them for the right reasons. Refusing surgery is not an easy option for any surgeon. If a patient is referred to me, I am expected to operate. But I have to also be sure that my decision is not motivated by ego or any personal or financial gain. There are times when I have to resist the temptation to operate – the referral pressure, the patient pressure, the financial pressure – and do the right thing, which is to *not* recommend surgery. In 'Primum Non Nocere: First, Do No Harm', we will talk about ethics. It is one of the very first lessons you learn in medical school.

Another way of understanding risk is to assess how sure you are before taking one. In *Get Out of Your Own Way,*[1] Robert Cooper talks about how the US Marine Corps deal with decision paralysis. They use a technique called Decision Tempo in which they go ahead and make a decision if they have a '70 per cent solution'; that is, if the decision maker has 70 per cent

---

1   Robert K. Cooper, *Get Out of Your Own Way: The 5 Keys to Surpassing Everyone's Expectations*, New York: Crown Business, 2006

information and is 70 per cent confident that the decision will be executed successfully. This theory can also be used wonderfully for taking smart risks. Are you 70 per cent sure? Good enough.

But it isn't always easy. In August 1986, a woman in labour was in my clinic and her contractions were progressing slowly, the foetal heart sounds punctuated by the sound of the pouring rain. Had this been any other case on any other day, I would have been as involved, but perhaps a little more clinical and dispassionate. But that day was a bit special because the woman in labour was my wife. And she was about to deliver what would be my first child.

There is plenty of debate on operating or treating family or close friends because of the emotional costs involved, but the general consensus was that I should not have been anywhere near the OT. When emotions get entangled with clinical procedure, it is a riskier way to work. Even my mother-in-law and my mother, who were waiting outside that day, wondered if I'd be able to do this. I overheard them talking – in grave and dubious tones – about whether *I* should have been the doctor to deliver the baby or whether it should have been someone else. Not very flattering.

But while there are no medical codes on this in India, I believed that given my profession, if I could not trust myself to deliver my own child, how could I ask anyone else to trust me to deliver theirs?

But as my wife's labour progressed and she was fully dilated, things started to go wrong. The baby's heart rate started dipping significantly and consistently which meant that the baby was in trouble. Suddenly, what seemed like a smooth delivery so far quickly spiralled into a crisis situation. The baby's heartbeat – my own *child's* heartbeat – was fading and it had to be delivered *immediately*. The only decision was how. I had to decide if I needed do a caesarean-section or use a vacuum cup. A C-section would have taken minutes which I did not have. I had to take a call. I applied the vacuum cup and pulled, but the foetal heart sounds were still slow.

No change.

I began sweating. My thoughts began to stray. I began to doubt my decision to not opt for a C-section, but I had to stay in the game. I tried again. I pulled and my wife pushed, I pulled some more and the vacuum slipped. I immediately applied the outlet forceps and delivered the child. The baby cried immediately. It was a girl.

I was holding my daughter in my arms. My first-born.

I don't think I have ever experienced such joy.

When emotions mix with medical decision-making, whether it is treating close relatives, celebrities or powerful people, it is always a far riskier proposition. But if I had listened to those around me, I wouldn't have been able to deliver my own daughter which would have been something I would have always regretted.

Four years later, I delivered my son.

The most unsettling part about risks is also the most exciting: we are unable to predict the future and we are unable to control it. We can look to the past, yes, for a better understanding of what we need to do for the way forward, but it can only be a limited understanding. But what if the outcome is better than we thought it would be? Without exception, all patients expect us to have certainty in our clinical examination, certainty in investigations and certainty in the outcome of surgery. Yes, you have to prepare as thoroughly as you can and take calculated risks, but the truth of it all is that nothing is certain. When we as specialists tell patients that we are not certain about the diagnosis or we give a differential diagnosis, it is taken to mean that there is lack of knowledge or expertise on the doctor's part, which is not usually the case. This sometimes prompts physicians to impress patients by their certainty in diagnosis; and false certainty can do tremendous damage. It is recklessness.

While it is an essentially human need to cling to certainty, we have to live with uncertainty. And it is this comfort with uncertainty that gives one the confidence to leap into a potentially exciting unknown.

Take that leap. It is only when you jump that you can learn how to fly.

The Bare Bones

LIFE LESSONS

From this chapter, you now know that

- Risk taking is something that even the most successful people in the world have in common. Quite simply, no risk, no reward.

- There is a difference between risk and recklessness.

- Stratify your risk with the help of information, research and due diligence. Separate the risks you take into high-risk and low-risk.

- You will never be 100 per cent sure. Move ahead even if you're 70 per cent confident.

- Take risks for the right reasons. And you will know what those reasons are.

What Do You Do Now?

6 **Develop an appetite for risk.** If you are very risk averse, start by taking smaller meaningless risks like watching a movie without seeing the review or taking the initiative on smaller low-profile projects at work like organizing a farewell for your boss. The purpose, of course, is to inculcate a taste for risk and to slowly graduate to taking more high-profile roles like leading projects that the CEO has an interest in or introducing a product on a larger scale. Needless to say, the higher the risk, the more risk stratification you would have to practise and the more calculated the risk. But take them. And do note that with an appetite for risk, you need to inculcate an appetite for failure as well. Be aware. Be prepared.

CHAPTER EIGHT

Medical Specialization
AND WHAT WE CAN LEARN

Not so long ago, the patients waiting in hospital OPDs had fewer corridors to get lost in. Cancer patients would simply go to general oncologists, heart patients would go to cardiologists and the overenthusiastic sixty-year-old – who decided to relive his youth by getting on to a motorcycle and subsequently breaking his ankle – would have to deal with a general orthopaedic doctor. And, of course, his wife. Even fifty years ago, an MBBS degree would be the end to the journey of medicine, with an MS or MD as optional requirements. But now, as we all know, even an MS or MD is not the end. It is only the beginning.

The number of medical specialties have now exploded and patients sometimes have to see different doctors for the same problem, depending on the scale and the duration of the treatment. An average cancer patient will probably now be seen by not one, but sometimes at least four doctors: the primary physician – who could be a specialist in the area where the cancer has been discovered – along with a medical oncologist, a radiologist and an onco surgeon. To illustrate how specialized medicine has now become, orthopaedic doctors are now divided into general orthopaedics, knee replacement surgeons, shoulder surgeons, hip replacement surgeons, spine surgeons and now there is also an entire super specialty dedicated to bone cancers that are treated by orthopaedic oncologists. It is rumoured that knee surgeons may soon be divided into left and right knees.

From a single point approach, where your friendly neighbourhood 'family doctor' was the one you called for almost everything, medical conditions are now treated using the super specialty approach and the race is on amongst doctors to specialize in smaller and smaller areas, to be the *God of Small Things*[1]. Finding a specialty – or a signature skill – is the cornerstone of most budding doctors. It is the question that most hangs over their heads. You no longer ask a medical student if they want to be a cardiologist, for example. You may want to ask if they would like to be a cardiothoracic surgeon, an interventional cardiologist or a paediatric cardiologist. The age of the generalist is now over.

---

1   Arundhati Roy, *The God of Small Things*, New York: Random House, 1997

And it is not just important to specialize, it is also crucial to be extremely good at it. If you are indeed attempting to be the 'God of Small Things', the operative word here is *God*. Or at least somewhere close.

To be a good laparoscopic surgeon, laparoscopic suturing – stitching inside the body with just cameras and telescopes to guide you – is a crucial step that needs practiced hand-eye coordination. Aspiring laparoscopic surgeons cannot perform advanced surgeries unless they are extremely proficient in laparoscopic suturing. It would take me hours and hours on a day-to-day basis for months to improve my laparoscopic stitching skills. Over time, I had practiced enough to start showing other doctors how to stitch, to the point where I was noticed by two surgeons from Singapore in 1996 at a conference in Mumbai during a demonstration I was giving. This led to an invite to train delegates at an international conference at Singapore the following year. This led to more training and faculty invites, both in India and around the world. This then led to my having the confidence to contest and be elected to represent Asia for three years on the board of the International Society for Gynecologic Endoscopy.

It all started with the smallest thing of all. A stitch. A much-practiced skill that became my signature simply because I had done it over and over again.

While medicine has clearly defined specialties, identifying and developing niche areas in other careers might be a little trickier. I needed to work hard on my skill of laparoscopic suturing because it was important for me to excel at it as I could then hone what is now my super specialty – an expertise in laparoscopic surgery with a focus on fibroid surgeries or myomectomies (myoma = fibroid and ectomy = removal) and hysterectomies.

Think about how this applies to you. Imagine if you have these one or two superlative skills which set you apart, a way of working that you are known for so much so that when someone thinks of a specific problem, you are the first name that pops up in their mind. Think of the professional, prestige and financial implications of being the master of your domain.

Mastering a niche is also a more efficient way to work. When you start practising a new skill, it takes a relatively longer amount of time to work on it. But as you get better, you start taking lesser and lesser time to get the same results. And that — as we discussed in 'The Science of Change' — is just the way your brain works: your amygdala loves automating processes through the formation of habits. So that you barely need to think about what you are doing. It took me, for example, four hours to do my first laparoscopic procedure, something I now wrap up in forty-five minutes. Brian Tracy, in his book *The Focal Point*, has mapped out the Law of Increasing Return when you focus on perfecting your signature craft. Look at how the time taken per activity decreases every time you do it, until you reach the optimum time you take.

Your signature skill (signature = unique to you, skill = ability or expertise) is your unique, and in this case professional, fingerprint that few can replicate. But if you haven't found that one skill or passion that showcases your innate talent, you are not alone. In *Now, Discover Your Strengths*, Marcus Buckingham and Donald Clifton speak of research conducted by the Gallup organization which asked 1,98,000 employers spread over 7,939 business units in thirty-six companies one simple question: 'At work, do you have the opportunity to do what you do best every day?'

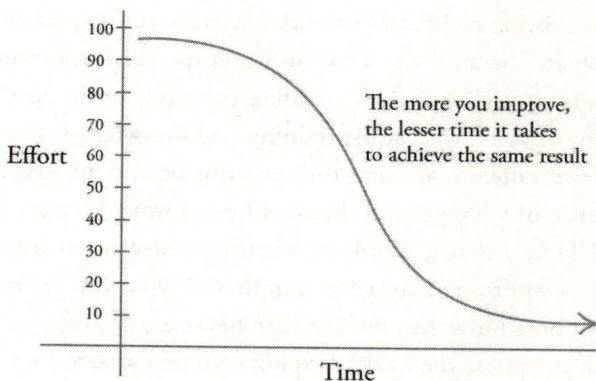

The more you improve, the lesser time it takes to achieve the same result

Time versus Effort: The Law of Increasing Return

The answer was that the majority – 80 per cent – of respondents felt that they were doing things that *didn't* play to their strengths. As Marcus Buckingham concluded, 'The real tragedy of life is not that each of us doesn't have enough strengths, it is that we fail to use the ones we have.'

Do we even know that we are *not* working in the skill-zone of our choice? Do we even know that we don't know? And if you know that where you are isn't where you want to be, how should you get there? Buckingham goes on to elaborate the three things you need to figure out and build your signature skill: talent, skill and knowledge. To identify your signature skill, first identify your most powerful **talent**. Are you more quantitatively inclined or creatively bent? Are you better at writing than organizing? Do you prefer leadership roles over solo projects? Once you have an idea of where your talents lie, put it in its context: how important, for example, is the skill of writing to your existing company? Would that make you move from a job heavy in operations to a role in the corporate communications department? Keeping the context in mind, shore up this raw talent of yours with **skills** training and **knowledge**. Raw talent is never enough, and not only has this been reiterated in 'The Science of Change' and 'Lessons Learnt from Medical Rigour' and 'The Pursuit of Mastery', this is also a truth you will always confront. Your genes can dictate what you are naturally predisposed towards, but they can never guarantee success. Not until you put in the work to exploit your potential to its potential. As I said before, the best surgeons aren't always the most intelligent, but they are always the most driven.

While all of this sounds simple enough, it is not always easy to identify your unique contribution to the world. It takes time, it takes honesty, it takes patience and it takes clarity – clarity in thought, process and action. Sometimes it even involves taking a plunge without thinking and meandering into areas that you later realize aren't suited to you. Dipping your toes in failure could be a great way to identify your success. But when you find your calling, there is no better feeling in this world; you know why you are here and what you were born to do.

You can start identifying your talents by asking yourself what makes you happy. In his book, Buckingham also talks about Warren Buffet addressing students at the University of Nebraska where he was quoted saying, 'I may have more money than you, but money doesn't make the difference. If there is any difference between you and me, it may simply be that I get up and have a chance to do what I love to do, every day. If you learn anything from me, this is the best advice I can give you.'[2] When identifying your signature skill, it is said that a good way to start is to shortlist the things that excite you, that enthral you, that greatly motivate you. Or is it? Sometimes the idea of love-what-you-do-do-what-you-love is all well and good. But is it practical?

Love what you do.

That is a lot of pressure.

The problem with the word 'love' is that it conjures up heavier connotations of devotion, deep involvement and even obsession. It is a big word. While some people find their passions early on, passions can also *develop*. If you can't find something you love, at least *like* what you do. Like a good relationship, sometimes love develops over time. 'Like' is a good-enough starting point, but it is something that is often missed by new-age maximizers who want to immediately find that elusive dream job.

Love what you do.

Failing which, *like* what you do.

Life is too short to be stuck doing something you hate.

Choosing something you do *not* love is a travesty of your time and energy. Or choosing something for the wrong reasons will not guarantee happiness for too long. A career that uses a skill which makes you money but makes you dread going in to work may be short-lived, wasting the time you could have used to develop another skill. Which is not to say that you may not have financial constraints or the need to put food on the table,

---

2 http://www.azquotes.com/quote/1248130; Last Accessed on 18 May 2016

precisely why you may work in roles you don't like. But your chances of being excellent – and therefore making money in the long run – at something you dislike are slim.

The ideal situation would be to choose an autotelic (auto = self, telic = goals) goal. Where you pursue the goal for the love of the goal itself. Where scaling heights in that goal is all the reward you need. When you do something purely for fame, power or money, you can never achieve mastery over it[3] because you are focusing on the outcome, not the process. Keep in mind that you experience only a fleeting glimpse of the outcome, but the process is what you have to live with. It is only when you learn a skill that you are very passionate about, will you achieve excellence.[4] The money will follow.

Find your kingdom. Choose your throne.

The Bare Bones

Life Lessons

From this chapter, you now know that

- The more you refine your signature skill, the better you get at it and the less time it takes to get the job done.

- Perfecting a signature skill is hard work. It takes practice, practice and more practice.

- If you haven't found your unique talent or calling, don't

---

3   Marcus Buckingham, and Donald O. Clifton, *Now, Discover Your Strengths: How to Develop Your Talents and Those of the People You Manage,* London: Pocket, 2005

4   Ibid

give up. Keep chipping away until you get there because when you find what you are meant to do in this world, there is no better feeling.

- Love what you do. Failing which, *like* what you do. 'Like' is an excellent starting point.

- Commercial consideration should *never* be the primary consideration when choosing your signature skill.

- Life is too short to be stuck doing something you hate.

What Do You Do Now?

7 Know Your Strengths. Make a leisurely list of all the things you like to do as well as all the things you think you are good at. Also note down on to this list things you think you would be good at like photography or writing, even if it is not what you do now or have never tried. From this list, shortlist the things that you can make a profession out of and what skills you need to develop to make it a viable career. **But the starting point should always be your talents and your desires. You never know where this simple exercise may lead you.**

CHAPTER NINE

Medical Teams
AND WHAT WE CAN LEARN FROM THEM

Over Christmas in the UK in 2004, Elaine Bromiley's[1] face had started to swell up, a symptom connected to the sinus problems that had dogged her for many years. She was advised minor surgery to straighten and correct the inside of her nose. Her husband Martin, a pilot, was familiar with this procedure, but indirectly: pilots frequently had battles with their sinuses – an occupational hazard from the constant changes in air pressure – and he knew of colleagues who had undergone similar procedures. He wasn't too worried, but as he and their two children, aged five and six, kissed her goodbye before her surgery, little did they know it would be the last time they would see her awake. Or, subsequently, alive. Due to complications from the surgery, Elaine Bromiley slipped into a coma from which she never emerged.

---

1   http://www.newstatesman.com/2014/05/how-mistakes-can-save-lives; Last Accessed on 18 May 2016

Investigations then revealed that Elaine had died at the hands of extremely experienced medical professionals who had over fifty years of experience between them; it was all because of a simple mistake. About two minutes into the operation, Elaine's airway collapsed, depriving her of oxygen. After repeatedly trying to ventilate the airway and failing, the anaesthesiologist called for help. It came in the form of an ENT surgeon and a senior anaesthesiologist and together, the three doctors worked to intubate Elaine, a procedure that involved the insertion of a tube into the airway, opening up the passage so that oxygen could be reintroduced into the lungs.

The three doctors couldn't get past an unidentifiable blockage in her airway and could not successfully intubate. There is a standard emergency in anaesthesia called 'Can't Ventilate, Can't Intubate', where if there is a situation in which neither ventilation nor intubation is possible, the next immediate thing to do is to surgically make a hole in the windpipe – called a tracheostomy – to force the air in. You don't waste time trying to intubate.

But in Elaine's case, the doctors went on trying to intubate. Time was running out.

Our bodies cannot survive without oxygen for too long and if we don't have enough, our brain functions start to slow down, the heart finds it difficult to beat and life starts to ebb away. Ten minutes is the medically prescribed window for oxygen deprivation after which the damage could be fatal.

In Elaine's case the doctors kept trying to intubate. The monitors were all pointing to signs of oxygen deprivation and depressed heartbeat. And even if they didn't notice that, Elaine's face was turning blue. But the three doctors still did not abort intubation. Ten minutes became fifteen which then became twenty. After twenty-five minutes, they finally succeeded in intubating her.

But it was too late.

Elaine had been without oxygen for too long and had severe brain damage. She was put into a medically induced coma to prevent her brain from swelling up. She was put on life support, but soon, after consulting with her husband, the doctors took her off that as well.

She died a week later. From a routine procedure.

On the face of it, this is a prime example of medical error. The doctors were so fixated with the task in front of them that they failed to step back and put things in perspective. This was a classic 'fixation error' – which we will go into greater detail in the chapter 'Lessons Learnt from Medical Mistakes' – where in a crisis situation, the brain's perceptual field shrinks, it starts to become obsessed with solving problems it thinks it can solve in order to stay in control, thus losing track of almost everything else. But this is not why I bring this story to you.

During the time that they were trying to intubate Elaine, the nurses present noticed Elaine's face turning blue, the plummeting of her oxygen levels, her erratic blood pressure and her breathing. When later asked, they said they had been surprised that the doctors weren't attempting a tracheotomy, but didn't voice their concerns. One nurse actually handed over a tracheotomy set to the doctors, but was ignored. Another nurse called the ICU and tried to book a bed. They tried to signal their apprehension, but were overlooked.

They didn't signal loudly enough.

That is how a team should *not* work.

Surgery is never done alone and needs a specialized team to facilitate it. Every surgery is like a live performance – maybe that is why it is said that the conventional term for an operation room is 'theatre'! A conventional laparoscopic surgery, which typically lasts for sixty minutes, needs the help of at least three specialties – surgery, anaesthesiology and nursing – and a list of specialized equipment in a carefully choreographed routine. But the team assisting the surgeon also serves as extra pairs of eyes to catch what he or she might be missing during the operation. That is how it works. In theory, at least.

But in practice that is not how it always works, unfortunately. Depending on the hospital, medicine can be one of the most hierarchical professions that exist. Dissent, insubordination and the crossing of boundaries are not encouraged and juniors are hesitant to point out errors. The nurses in Elaine's case probably didn't feel it was their place to alert the doctors of their error – even though they made tentative attempts to do so – which turned out to have a fatal outcome. In yet another infamous case, a young medical student alerted the surgeons that they were operating on the wrong kidney, but she was ignored.[2] They removed the healthy one and the patient died from the diseased kidney six weeks later.

There is no shortage of hierarchical organizations, especially in India, where teams are still very conscious of seniority. But when people don't speak up, teams start to collapse or at the very least, they don't function to their full potential. When there is a team culture that renders those more junior down the chain

2   http://www.newstatesman.com/2014/05/how-mistakes-can-save-
    lives; Last Accessed on 18 May 2016

mute spectators for fear of displeasing their seniors, that is the beginning of the end for new thought, progress, experimentation or simply even efficiency. You can make mistakes no matter how senior you are.

NO ONE IS TALKING TO EACH OTHER

In 2007, the American Joint Commission's annual report on quality and safety discovered that insufficient communication between healthcare providers, or between providers and the patients and family members contributed to over half of the serious adverse events in accredited hospitals. Other prominent causes included insufficient assessment of the patient's condition as well as poor leadership and training. This implies that millions of patients in the US die because of:

- The lack of proper communication
- An improper assessment of a patient's condition
- Poor leadership
- Deficient training

So many preventable deaths.
Simply caused because no one is talking to each other.

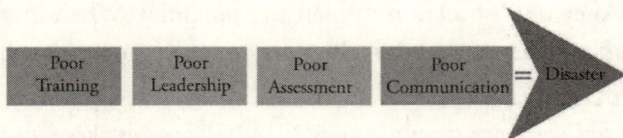

| Poor Training | Poor Leadership | Poor Assessment | Poor Communication | = Disaster |

This doesn't mean that teams don't need leaders. They do. But in Elaine's case, the doctors themselves were not in charge: there was no clear leader and the nurses followed the hierarchical line. Nobody was leading and nobody was speaking up. There was a complete breakdown of communication.

Yet, teams are crucial to the achievement of your dreams. Nothing of importance, significance or value can be achieved alone. Even those seemingly operating in isolation, like sport stars and other celebrities, have teams of agents, publicists, stylists, trainers, coaches and managers working quietly behind the scenes. But what is a *good* team? How can it be defined? **A good team is one where you put people with different or complementary skill sets together with a view to achieve a common purpose.** A good team is bound by a shared commitment towards attaining the same goal. When a team is functioning at its highest level, the collective needs of a good team is *greater* than the singular need of an individual, especially the individual in charge of that team.

A good team is also one in which team members are not vilified for making mistakes if there is an environment that is deeply critical of failure. Dr Victor Trastek, CEO of the Mayo Clinic, Arizona, works on the principle of 'teach, don't blame'. He says that when things go wrong, errors should be seen as something to learn from. While this approach doesn't always realistically prevent the practice of blame games, you can never go wrong with a constructive, democratic approach in the long run.

Good teams also have good leaders. It is the job of the leader to set the team culture, navigate discussions, listen openly and get the best out of the team. It is also the leader's responsibility to ensure the clear definition of roles. Which is why a team is as good – or bad – as the person who leads it.

Smooth Surgery

Surgical teams can teach you a lot about working together. Good surgical teams:

1. **Trust Each Other**: Good surgical teams are open about their mistakes and problems and are also open to asking for help.

2. **Know How to Disagree**: These teams are marked by mature discussions, healthy disagreements and know how to manage differences of opinion.

3. **Are Committed to a Collective Goal**: That of saving – or improving the quality – of a human life.

4. **Are Focused on Results**: Surgical team members are incredibly committed to the good outcome of the procedure and work in tandem to ensure it.

The credo of the Mayo Clinic in the United States is 'Teamwork Isn't Optional'; there is a belief that doctors from different specialties should work together collaboratively and selflessly to treat patients. For example, if a patient needed simple surgery but is diabetic and a heart patient, the consulting surgeon, the cardiologist, the anaesthesiologist and the diabetologist should work together to ensure that all the boxes are ticked before the patient is wheeled in for surgery. India is seeing this happen as well. Cancer patients are now being seen by a *panel* of doctors – called a tumour board – right from radiologists, medical oncologists, surgical oncologists, histopathologists and other doctors from specialties relevant to the patient's condition. It is not always easy to get doctors to meet together to collaboratively counsel and work on a single patient, but these paradigm shifts are being seen here as well.

When constructing your team, how creatively and efficiently can you manage the resources that you have? Can you bypass multiple hierarchies? Can you mine specialized skill sets in ways that bring the team a sort of collective benefit? Putting a team together is an art in itself. You need optimum numbers to work efficiently – not too many but not too few – and balance the right skills to get the optimum number of perspectives. You also *do* need a chain of command – you need leaders, but you also need foot soldiers – so long as the purpose of the team isn't sacrificed at the altar of hierarchy. It was Halford E. Luccock who said, *'No one can whistle a symphony. It takes an orchestra to play it.'* It is important to keep fine-tuning the process of making your team.

The more a team works together, the better they get. The sequence of individual tasks that makes up a surgery becomes so automatic and instinctive that team members sometimes don't even need words to signal the start of a new stage in the procedure; a simple nod is enough. When I go out of town to operate, or work in other OTs, I take some essential team members with me because it is more efficient than getting used to new team members and the unique ways in which they work. But these are older, well-oiled teams.

But old or new, whatever the team may be, the key element is always *trust*. From mistrust springs close-mindedness, fear and the inability to speak up. Study after study has consistently shown the relationship between poor communication among healthcare workers and preventable medical errors, as Elaine's case will tell you. Communicate. Talk to each other. Get used to either leading or being a part of a team. Because as you go up the ranks, you will find yourself almost always being a part of one in some form or another. And that is because, as John Maxwell puts it so well, *'One is too small a number to achieve greatness.'*

The Bare Bones

Life Lessons

From this chapter, you now know that

- Nothing of any significance can be achieved alone. You need a team and you need one that works well.

- Good teams are:

  o Democratic, open and encourage feedback and trust.

  o Don't vilify members for mistakes.

  o Have a diverse mix of complementary skill sets.

  o Bound by a shared goal and a shared commitment towards that goal.

  o As good as their leader.

- When a team is functioning at its highest level, the collective needs of a good team is *greater* than the singular need of an individual, especially the individual in charge.

- Put a lot of thought into how you want to construct your team. It could be one of the most important professional decisions you will ever make.

What Do You Do Now?

8 **Identify Your Weaknesses.** This is an exercise of complete insight and honesty and is the *first* part of constructing a team: finding people who have what you don't. To better understand that, first make a note of the qualities and skills that you *lack*. Second, fit names to that list. Think of who will be able to fill in the gaps and bring to the table what you *cannot*. This exercise will help construct the beginnings of a great team, the beginnings of a successful innings.

CHAPTER TEN

Lessons Learnt from Medical Mistakes

In medicine, things don't always work out as you planned, neither for patients nor for doctors. A thirty-nine-year-old woman went in for a scheduled hysterectomy, but died on the operating table instead. Her post-mortem revealed that instead of putting the endotracheal tube in her windpipe, the anaesthesiologist put it into her oesophagus, the food pipe.[1] The Rhode Island Hospital in the United States had the dubious distinction of operating on the wrong side of patients' brains – in a class of surgical error known as wrong site surgery – three times. It is important to mention here that it was three times in the *same* year.[2]

---

1 http://www.medscape.com/features/slideshow/med-errors; Last Accessed 18 May 2016
2 Ibid

In yet another case, a pregnant woman suffering from low potassium levels brought on by dehydration due to vomiting and nausea went to the hospital, only to never return. To bump her potassium levels back up, the nurse administered it intravenously, i.e., through a drip. But she miscalculated and overshot the dosage. The patient died within the hour.

Medicine saves lives, but it can also be what takes them away. The role of medical error in fatalities cannot be ignored, no matter how much we, as doctors and patients, want to close our eyes. At the time of going to press, according to researchers at Johns Hopkins, deaths due to medical mistakes was the *third* biggest killer in the United States, exceeded only by heart disease and cancer.[3]

All these deaths are senseless.

Most of these deaths can be prevented.

Despite all the training, the techniques and the technology, medical error seems to be an intrinsic part of medical practice. Doctors are sometimes treated – and sometimes even *want* to be treated – like God. But as renowned public health researcher and surgeon Dr Atul Gawande says, 'It (medicine) is an imperfect science, an enterprise of constantly changing knowledge, uncertain information, fallible individuals and at the same time lives on the line.'[4] Medicine has both astounding successes and horrifying failures.

---

3   https://www.dotmed.com/news/story/30695?p_begin=1; Last Accessed on 18 May 2016

4   Atul Gawande, *Complications: A Surgeon's Notes On an Imperfect Science*, New York: Metropolitan Books, 2002

The statistics aren't very comforting either.[5] About a quarter of all patients – 25 per cent or one in four – develop complications post-surgery. The overall mortality rate is about 0.5–5 per cent for major surgery. And – you should sit down for this – *half* of all the adverse cases in hospitalized patients were connected to problems related to surgical care. And *half* of these adverse results of surgery were thought to be preventable.

That is one in every two patients.

But why does this happen? And can something be done to prevent it? In his seminal book, *The Checklist Manifesto* – which describes the use of simple checklists for preventable medical errors – Atul Gawande states it can. He further elaborates that there are two kinds of errors. The first are errors due to *ignorance* stemming from not knowing enough; this is especially relevant for interns, junior doctors and residents. The second are errors due to *ineptitude* or negligence; this is not concerned with a lack of knowledge, but the deeper, more problematic situation of not applying that knowledge correctly. Errors due to ineptitude can be further classified into slips and lapses. A slip is an error owing to distraction. A lapse is an error owing to the failure of memory. Senior doctors, surgeons and nursing staff are more prone to errors of ineptitude.

The canvas on which these errors operate is a big one. According to a study in Israel, patients in an ICU are exposed to 178 individual processes or actions every day that include administering injections, medications, suction, oxygen and being

---

5   'Safe Surgery', http://www.who.int/patientsafety/safesurgery/en/; Last Accessed on 30 June 2016

hooked onto monitors. That is 178 actions. Or 178 possibilities for error. For the purposes of this chapter, though, we will not talk about errors due to ignorance because inexperience is a part of the learning curve in every profession and is not always preventable, unfortunately, even though they have consequences of their own. We will be concerned with errors made due to ineptitude, the most preventable of them all, for the purposes of understanding what goes behind the making of an error.

It is said that hindsight is a perfect science. When you look back on your mistakes and try to understand how you could have done things differently, it suddenly all becomes perfectly clear. But when you're deep in the middle of a situation, the brain has different ways of responding which could make humans more prone to error. But how can this be addressed? In Joseph T. Hallinan's landmark book, *Errornomics*, 70 per cent of airline errors, 90 per cent of car accidents and another 90 per cent of workplace accidents are ascribed to human error. However, while it is extremely useful to identify the cause, the problem is that once an error has been defined as a consequence of human fallibility, all further investigation stops. In fact, it should actually be the beginning of understanding how and why humans make mistakes.

In the paper published in the *Journal of Minimally Invasive Gynaecology* called 'Avoiding Complications of Laparoscopic Surgery: Lessons from Cognitive Science and Crew Resource Management', the authors reviewed errors in twenty-two unedited videos of laparoscopic gall bladder surgeries – called laparoscopic cholecystectomies – that ended in litigation. Only 3 per cent of the videos that were reviewed showed signs of technical or knowledge-based errors. A massive **97 per cent** of errors were caused due to visual or perceptual problems.[6]

How the Brain Makes Mistakes

The brain can trick you into making mistakes. When forty-year-old Tara walked in to my office complaining of abdominal pain, we decided to do a laparoscopy to check the cause. As she had had two surgeries prior to this, we were expecting scar tissue or adhesions. When we started the surgery, we were right: scar tissue had developed to the point that the fatty part of the bowel or intestine that is called the omentum was stuck to a part of the abdominal wall, causing the patient a great deal of pain. This is a complication that can sometimes occur after abdominal or laparoscopic surgeries in the area.

I began to slowly and carefully separate the omentum and the abdominal wall, ensuring that the intestine was not affected. After snipping for a few minutes, I pulled back the telescope and saw that what I was most trying to avoid had been done. I had snipped off a bit of the bowel as well. Undetected, this kind of mistake can cause serious infections or sepsis, peritonitis, leaking of faecal matter into the body and possibly death. I repaired it without any real complication arising from it and the patient recovered in three days.

But a mistake is still a mistake. What had gone wrong? Once I reviewed the tapes, I found that I was so focused on the fatty

---

6   W.H. Parker, A. Johns and J. Hellige, 'Avoiding Complications of Laparoscopic Surgery: Lessons from Cognitive Science and Crew Resource Management', *The Journal of Minimally Invasive Gynaecology*, May-June; 14 (3) (2007): 379-88

tissue – the omentum – that I had failed to notice the presence of the bowel, leading me to make a mistake. The video clearly showed that it was in my field of vision, but I had missed it entirely.

I fell prey to tunnel vision.

In understanding error, it is simple enough. Once the brain sees an image and determines its meaning, the brain preserves it in spite of the information that is contrary to this meaning.[7] The brain receives eleven million individual bits of perceptual information[8] *every second*. But in this overwhelming traffic, only forty bits are consciously processed. Sometimes, we miss things.

I could only see the omentum and not the bowel under it. Had the patient been closed up without me or my team noticing it, the consequences could have been fatal. Although tunnel vision errors result in death in few other professions, the larger question is this – when we are focused on only one aspect of our career, are we losing an understanding of the context? Are we losing perspective? Are we only seeing the small picture and not the bigger one? Are we losing sight of our long-term goals? Or are we simply focusing on the means and not the end? Will what we are doing now matter in five, ten or even fifteen years?

A cousin of tunnel vision is the fixation error. You've probably encountered it. It seems unassuming enough and suddenly emerges in exam rooms, boardrooms, OTs and cockpits, sometimes with fatal outcomes. A fixation error creeps up on you in times of extreme stress. Say you are taking an online test

---

7   Ibid

8   Ibid

with multiple questions and you've been doing well so far until you encounter an extremely difficult question. You fixate over this question, agonizing over what the answer could be. You're *so close* to the answer that you can almost taste it. Before you realize it, minutes and not seconds have ticked by; you have been *stuck* on one question for too long. You panic and your brain goes into overdrive trying to solve it. You've spent so much time on it, you now rationalize, that you may as well see it through to the end, right?

Wrong.

Under stressful conditions, the brain's perceptual field sometimes shrinks and you become extremely focused on the need to solve what is exactly in front of you, where your field of attention has been drastically narrowed. You start to lose the perception of time, threat or consequence. You become *stuck* on a particular problem. Before you realize it, you're at the end of the exam and you don't even know how you got there.

But the more serious fixation errors have killed.

In late December 1978,[9] United Airlines Flight 173, carrying 189 people, was beginning its descent into Portland International Airport. The landing gear was lowered, but it was followed by a strange sound, a thump, and the aircraft tilted slightly to the right. One of the landing gear indicator lights was not switching on, suggesting a possible malfunction. As the plane continued to orbit the airport, the in-flight crew notified the Air Traffic Control about the problem and at the same time, tried to understand whether the landing gear had been lowered or not.

---

9   http://www.newstatesman.com/2014/05/how-mistakes-can-save-lives; Last Accessed on 18 May 2016

Almost half an hour later, while still orbiting Portland airport, the captain contacted the United Airlines maintenance centre, informing them that they would continue to circle for another fifteen to twenty minutes. At that point, there were 7,000 lbs of fuel aboard, about halfway down from the time the captain first radioed ATC. The crew on board still continued to debate about whether the landing gear was down.

As they continued to mull over the problem, they were losing their perception of time. And with the loss of time, there was another critical factor to go with it: the loss of fuel. They were losing fuel faster than they realized and suddenly it was too late. At seven minutes past the hour, the first engine shut down. Six minutes later, the other one followed suit. Their last message to the Air Traffic Control was, 'We're going down. We're not going to be able to make it to the airport.' They crashed into a wooded area in the suburbs of Portland.

Ten people lost their lives.

And all for nothing.

As it turned out in the ensuing investigation, the landing gear was down the entire time.

Fixation errors have been compared to a kind of 'momentary autism'[10] where single-mindedness becomes a compulsion in which your brain tells you to carry on with an activity even when you shouldn't. The consequences of this error can be especially fatal in the medical

10 W.H. Parker, A. Johns and J. Hellige, 'Avoiding Complications of Laparoscopic Surgery: Lessons from Cognitive Science and Crew Resource Management', *The Journal of Minimally Invasive Gynaecology*, May-June; 14 (3): 379-88, 2007

and airline industries; it is related to situations of extreme stress. But while fixation errors occur in high-stress situations, not all stress is bad. The Yerkes-Dodson Law measures the positive relationship between emotional arousal and level of performance. In other words, there is an actual optimum level of stress that helps you meet that deadline.

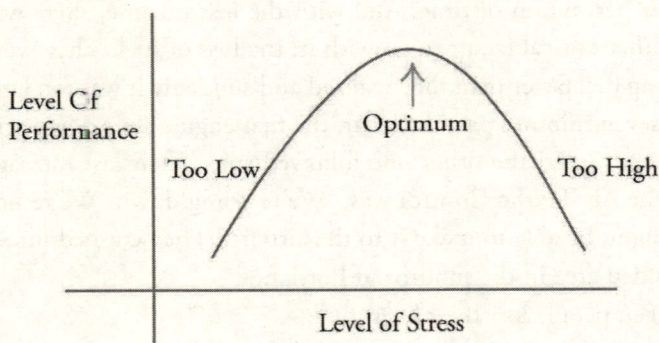

How Much Stress Is Good Stress? The Yerkes-Dodson Law

Good stress is the one I am currently undergoing, where a comfortable but looming deadline enables me to write this book sitting in the library in my hospital. At this point, I'm probably up to my optimum productivity; I am comfortably stressed knowing that I can finish this chapter today in time to write the next chapter tomorrow. But throw in a medical emergency, an unscheduled surgery, a couple of more urgent calls? Suddenly it is not so comfortable, and suddenly the deadline begins to loom larger.

However, how much stress you need to optimally perform depends entirely on you. For some, ten days before a deadline is tight and for others, it is a night before. While the level of stress is also related to the quantum of work, it is the individual who is best placed to decide at what point the stress becomes counterproductive. However, extreme levels of stress result in a performance decline because the brain does not correctly process the increase of incoming information which could lead to errors.[11] This kind of reaction from the brain is a common one. Extreme stress does not discriminate.

Nor does prolonged sleep deprivation. According to one study, being awake for twenty-four hours dramatically increased medical interns' tendency to make preventable medical mistakes by *double* and sometimes even *triple*, to include ones that could hurt or, worse, kill a patient.[12] The forty-hour work week is one of the basic laws of human productivity. The first four hours after waking up are seen as the most productive, but as the day goes on, the propensity to make mistakes is higher as focus and alertness fade away. As the day gets longer, irrespective of the industry, productivity suffers. This is a fact. One that has, to date, not been convincingly disputed.

Exhaustion adds to the propensity of error. Sixty-hour weeks are not just tiring, but they make the worker error- prone. The

11 W.H. Parker, A. Johns and J. Hellige, 'Avoiding Complications of Laparoscopic Surgery: Lessons from Cognitive Science and Crew Resource Management', *The Journal of Minimally Invasive Gynaecology*, May-June; 14 (3): 379-88, 2007

12 "Medical Errors', https://en.wikipedia.org/wiki/Medical_error#Healthcare_complexity; Last Accessed 30 June 2016

time you spend compensating for your mistakes could use up all the extra hours you put in at work, making it counterproductive. When I was a resident, I remember having worked for thirty-six hours at a stretch and then going into the operating room dizzy to perform a surgery. Skipping just one night's sleep noticeably impairs the brain's ability to work. And scientists have found that while we can work for longer stretches of time with little sleep, what gets sacrificed, increasingly, is the ability to think.

When tired, even the best workers start to work like the worst ones.

Charles Czeister, professor of sleep medicine at the Harvard Medical School, has said that going without sleep for twenty-four hours or sleeping for just four or five hours a night for over a week brings about an impairment that is equal to a blood alcohol level of 0.1 per cent. It is best to keep in mind that in India the legal limit for driving under the influence of alcohol is about 0.03 per cent.[13] If you're sleep deprived, you clearly don't have to be *drunk* to come in drunk to work.

Errors also happen due to hierarchy. In the chapter 'Medical Teams: And What We Can Learn From Them', we had highlighted incidents where this tendency to follow hierarchical lines had gone dangerously wrong. Simply put, seniors do not like juniors telling them what to do. Detailed in her book *Willful Blindness*[14], Margaret Heffernan says that the brain does not like

---

13 http://timesofindia.indiatimes.com/city/kolkata/Dont-drink-and-drive-cops-are-watching/articleshow/45406440.cms; Last Accessed on 18 May 2016

14 Margaret Heffernan, *Willful Blindness: Why We Ignore the Obvious at Our Peril*, New York: Walker & Co., 2012

conflict and prefers to resolve it. This could be why we prefer like-minded people. According to her, 'When we work hard to defend our core benefits, we risk becoming blind to the evidence that could tell us we're wrong.'[15]

And sometimes, plain and simple distractions can't be as plain and simple in consequence. Multiple experiments conducted by Dan Simons have concluded that we see only what we expect, which makes us *unable to see what we don't*. The brain can take in only so much at one time. 'For the human brain,' says Simons, 'attention is a zero sum game: if we pay more attention to one place, object or event, we necessarily pay less attention to others.' Simons further highlights this through the example of using hands-free devices while driving. The device is meaningless, he says. It is not about keeping your hands free, it is about keeping your *mind* free. It is the share of attention, the mental *resource* that is limited. Talking while driving is simply expecting too much of your brain.

While we have detailed some significant human errors that occur in medicine, is there a science to averting them? Can this question be extrapolated to our personal and professional lives and our families? And if we cannot avert errors, how do we detect them early on and manage them? Yes, we can learn that a good night's sleep is more important than we thought. We can learn to switch off the notifications and only answer our emails and texts when we have the time, limiting the distractions we face. We can also try and listen to comments and opinions with an open mind, no matter what the source, junior or senior. But what do we do under extreme stress? The brain takes over, doesn't it?

---

15 Ibid

Even in medical or aviation cases, stress can be put into perspective. If the crew of Flight 173 had just taken a few minutes to step out of the situation and check the fuel gauge, could the disaster have been averted? Could all those lives have been saved? Atul Gawande, in his landmark book *The Checklist Manifesto*, has outlined what can be done to prevent the preventable. He has worked with the World Health Organization (WHO) to create the Safe Surgery Checklist. Using the deceptively simple idea of a checklist before surgeries helps to create 'situation awareness' which is, as the name suggests, designed to ensure that the awareness of the operating environment is maintained. Generating awareness could include asking what the patient is being operated for, what may happen next, etc., in order to constantly focus the attention of the team on the surgery at hand. Members of the team are also encouraged to speak up during the process. This may seem simple, but do keep in mind that while surgeons are familiar with the cases they are operating on, the nurses and technicians may not be. In bigger hospitals, there are usually floating teams that assist on every operation, which is why briefing them is so vital. There have been cases in which members of the operating team didn't even know what the surgery was for – an enormous oversight when an extra pair of eyes could have prevented errors that have claimed so many.

There is also an accident causation model called the 'Swiss Cheese Model', developed by British psychologist James Reason, to explain why some of the bigger disasters occur – and it is not due to one reason, but many. It is due to many. Using Swiss cheese as an analogy where the holes of the cheese line up, errors sometimes occur when many things go wrong at once. For example, not only are you making a mistake, but your team doesn't point it out either. Or, to use another instance, if your patient is coding because of an extreme reaction to a drug and he dies not only because of the severe reaction to medication but also because the equipment to save him – like a defibrillator – was malfunctioning. Grave, serious error may not always occur until many unfortunate things happen at the same time.

Different kinds of software are being used to detect abnormal test results, keep a tab on medical orders and even detect allergies to medications. Technology can also be used to maintain schedules of maintenance for surgical equipment. And it is getting more sophisticated all the time. Whatever be the case, it is important that medical mistakes are not covered up. The Institute of Medicine (IOM) released an article 'To Err Is Human' which went on to establish that the larger problem with the issue of medical error is not that there is an abundance of bad people working in medicine, but that there are good people who are compelled to work in bad systems. And it is those very systems that need to be changed.

The medical fraternity has now come up with a set of 'Never Events', which, as the name suggests, includes certain errors that should *never* occur. The list includes operating on the wrong patient or the wrong limb or body part, errors in blood transfusion, mistakes caused due to incompetent surgeons or inadequate equipment at the start of an elective surgery. For easier reference, we've called it the 'Never Occur List' or NOL.

What does your NOL look like? In your personal/ family life and your professional life, what is your list of non-negotiables?

What Can We Learn from the WHO Safe Surgery Checklist?[16]

With a view to eliminating preventable medical errors, Dr Atul Gawande, together with the WHO, designed the Surgical Safety Checklist after it was discovered that many errors in the operating rooms were preventable. The checklist consists of safety checks designed to safeguard and improve the performance of the team in the operating room.

Team Briefing: All the members of the surgical team are required to attend a team briefing in the beginning to ensure that the requirements are understood as well as skill levels, staffing and equipment requirements are identified, and to also plan for any expected problems.

Sign In: The period before the administration of the anaesthesia enables the team to check the surgical site on the patient's body to ensure that it has been properly marked and all known allergies of the patient have been checked.

Time Out: Before making the first incision the entire team present in the theatre should introduce

16 https://www.rcseng.ac.uk/surgeons/surgical-standards/ professionalism-surgery/gsp/documents/the-high-performing-surgical-team-2013-a-guide-to-best-practice; Last Accessed on 20 May 2016

themselves, if it has not been already done. This encourages those present to identify any concerns at this stage.

Sign Out: Before the patient leaves the theatre, the team needs to ensure that instruments, sponges and needles have been accounted for to confirm that nothing has been left inside the patient's body.

Debriefing: All the members of the surgical team need to be a part of a final discussion at the end of the procedure to discuss the positives, the issues, the concerns and identify areas of improvement.

We cannot escape our fallibility and fragility. It is the essence of the human condition. We also cannot escape the limitations of human cognition, but once we accept it, we can begin to work towards consciously transcending it. Surgeons can age ten years in ten days if a patient has a complication resulting from their error. But it is also important to learn from the error. Flight 173 became a teaching case for airline pilots of what *not* to do, and of the three incidents of error mentioned at the start of this chapter, two were used[17] to transform the standard of care.

From those mistakes, many more lives have been saved.

---

17 http://www.medscape.com/features/slideshow/med-errors; Last Accessed on 18 May 2016

The Bare Bones

LIFE LESSONS

From this chapter, you now know that

- Making mistakes is an inescapable part of the human condition.

- Errors have many triggers:

    - You could make mistakes under **stress** which may lead to tunnel vision or fixation errors

    - You could make mistakes due to **sleep deprivation**

    - You could make mistakes because of **inattention**

- However, some of the biggest preventable disasters occur when many things go wrong at the same time, as detailed in the Swiss Cheese Model. Limit the possibility of error by ensuring the maintenance and efficiency of *every* contributing element.

- Attention is a zero-sum game. The more you multitask, the more error-prone you become.

- When you make mistakes, try and analyse why you made them. Self-awareness and self-assessment are crucial for the reduction in error. Always try to never make the same mistakes again.

- Learn to recover from your mistakes quickly and don't let them demoralize you.

- To err is human, to learn is divine.

What Do You Do Now?

9

Make Your Own NOL. Just like surgery has a Never Occur List (NOL) of medical errors, what is on *your* NOL? What are the mistakes you should *never* make? **Make a comprehensive NOL for both your personal and professional life.**

Part Three

THE COGNITIVE COMPONENT

CHAPTER ELEVEN

Cognition
I Think, Therefore I Am

The third and final component of success, i.e., cognition, is concerned with your belief system: how you see the world around you and its relationship to achieving what you set out to do. According to Robert E. Franken in *Human Motivation,* cognitive processes are concerned with knowing. And knowing in turn includes 'thinking, perceiving, abstracting, synthesizing, organizing or otherwise conceptualizing the nature of the external world and the self.'[1] Other definitions associate cognition with 'language, imagination, perception and planning'.[2] Quite simply, cognitive thinking for success involves believing that you can succeed.

---

1   Robert E., Franken, *Human Motivation,* 6th ed., Australia: Thomson/Wadsworth, 2007

2   http://psychology.about.com/od/cindex/g/def_cognition.htm; Last Accessed on 18 May 2016

While the first two parts of *The Anatomy of Success* were concerned with how you're biologically predisposed to succeed and how you can learn to be successful, *whether or not you believe you can succeed in the first place* will determine if you act on any information in these pages. In a sense, this part may have come right at the end, but belief is actually the starting point for any action.

Many people don't pick up the skills they need to get ahead because they don't believe they *can* get ahead. From the cognitive perspective, success needs a combination of burning ambition and optimism. To that end, 'Part 3' will be concerned with 'Volition: The Anatomy of the Want' and 'Wheel In, Walk Out: Lessons Learnt from Positive Thinking'.

Because how you think pretty much determines the choices you make.

CHAPTER TWELVE

Volition

THE ANATOMY OF THE WANT

You can take as many lessons as you want from this book and from others, from workshops, mentors, even from your mistakes. But none of this would be possible without a want, without a need to win above all else. While your biological component is predisposed to success and while you can learn successful habits, it is meaningless without the third component of success: that drive, that inner urge, that volition. Without volition, you can neither channel your biological gifts nor have the willingness to understand that there are things you need to change and learn in the first place. Without that deep-seated *desire* to change, there can be no change at all.

Research, according to Epstein in 1991 and Seligman in 1990, shows that success is not, in fact, about intelligence. It is instead, as they have elaborated, dependent on how we think about the world. In other words, volition – defined as will or desire – is *primary,* not secondary or tertiary.

To succeed, you need to desperately, truly, madly, deeply *want* to.

And that makes sense. In the concepts explored in this book, throughout the length and breadth of motivational theory, medicine and science from which have been culled lessons and examples, the way forward needs to be propelled by *something*. Without that spark, it is just firewood waiting to be lit. Scientists have concluded that this spark is simply our will, though not to be confused with willpower. It doesn't matter what we are born with or what our environment is, if we have the will to succeed, if we have the inner urge to do well and if we are willing to do whatever it takes to transcend obstacles, our chances of being successful increase considerably.

Yet, in science, the idea that humans have 'free will' is controversial. Many theorists and academics still believe that our genes can limit how good we can become or how or what we can learn to change. It has been concluded that change is still dictated by our genetic and environmental limitations and to change, we need to work *within* these limitations. For example, you can use deliberate practice, mirror neurons and peak performance as techniques to become very good at playing the piano, but you may not – because of your genetic make-up – be a concert pianist at the genius level. We can be good, but perhaps not brilliant And while we have addressed this point in 'The Science of Change', we have genes that can make us more predisposed to success, we should channel brain functions irrespective of what we were born with.

In his seminal work *Human Motivation,* Robert E. Franken has defined volition or will as a cognitive, i.e., thinking, process by which a human being decides and commits to doing something; an active and conscious decision *to be.* The concept of volition implies that you can create your own destiny. Inherent in its definition, volition means that there are very few things we *cannot* become. This includes becoming a concert-level pianist if that is what we decide and commit to being.

This concept shifts the focus of human ability from passive to *active.* Humans no longer have to respond to the world around them, but can create an entirely new world of their own; a new world for you, of you and by you. It is a place where you decide what you want to be, where you want to go and how you want to get there.

It is really about what you believe.

Creating Volition

Volition can be created, it can be nurtured and it can be developed. And this can be done, in one way, by creating a new self-concept. To understand what we mean by this term, Markus and Nurius[1] suggest that you can create a brand new self all on your own – the best possible you that, for example, goes for the gold, starts a company of your own and sells it for a billion dollars, finds someone to marry, has a child, is a good parent. You

---

1   Robert E. Franken, *Human Motivation*, 4th ed.,VrPacific Grove, CA: Brooks/Cole Pub. Co.,1998

then create strategies to help you *become* that self. This new self will then operate in a whole new world, doing new things, living a new life. This way of thinking, called the 'self-concept', is the starting point of the goals we set, the progress we make and the future we build for ourselves. Sometimes that inner urge, that desire itself needs to be *built*, and what better fountainhead than the blueprint of a self that is different from the one you are now?

To kick-start your volition, create a strong, inspiring, imaginative self-concept that sparks the urge or desire to succeed. But even in the creation of this new self-concept, we sometimes draw our blueprint from what we already know, from the domains we are already good at or the ones which use the talents we already have. That is when we need to introduce a whole new world into our concept of the self. Possibility. Or rather, limitless possibility. And define our self-concept as something that goes way beyond what we have ever imagined.

I'd like you to do a simple exercise: construct your new self-concept in the space below without giving it much thought. What are the qualities that you would like your new self to have? Stronger, smarter, a better boss, wife, husband, worker? Do it without thinking. Just blindly write them down.

_____

_____

_____

_____

_____

_____

_____

_____

Now do it again, but without your old context this time. Create a completely different self from the previous one; create two selves that don't resemble each other. Pen down the impossible. Write like nobody's reading.

I bet you would see a difference in both your self-concepts. The first one is probably a lot more conservative and more related to the life you have now, but just a better version of it. The second self-concept, I'm willing to bet, is different from the first. Maybe your second self-concept is brimming with all the qualities and talents you have been suppressing or never thought you had because you didn't think they were practical. Maybe the space has been left blank because you are unable to think of a world that has no limits.

What is stopping you?

In order to develop the best self-concept, we need to see the world differently. For example, instead of seeing threats, we should see challenges; instead of seeing problems, we should be seeing solutions. For example, research by Higgins in 1996 shows that by simply changing the way people viewed a situation from a threat to a challenge reduced the amount of stress. And multiple experiments by social psychologists show that by simply changing the way people label things, their perceptions and actions also undergo a change.[2] This, in turn, suggests that it may be possible for us to replace disabling thoughts with enabling ones. There is a term for this: it is called 'cognitive reframing' or 'restructuring'. Seeing things differently brings out a different reaction and possibly a different outcome. Some think that the world is their oyster, some think that the world is simply out to get them. What do you want the world to be?

---

2   Robert E. Franken, *Human Motivation*, 4th ed., VrPacific Grove, CA: Brooks/Cole Pub. Co.,1998.

But whatever self-concept you develop, do it for the right reasons. In his book *Drive,* Daniel Pink[3] categorized people into two types – Type X and Type I. Type X were those motivated by *extrinsic* desires like money, power, position, fame and prestige while Type I was classified as those motivated by *intrinsic* desires like learning for the sake of learning, goals for the sake of self-actualization or doing something purely for the passion of it, although Type I also does expect to be compensated adequately. It is much more motivating, Pink says, to function from intrinsic rather than extrinsic desire. This is further supported by Pink's research, where it was concluded that Type I almost always outperformed Type X. It corroborates the point that we have been making through this book – choose something you love to do, and not for the trappings of money or fame. You will be much more motivated to work and succeed, and the money will come to you in the end.

Revel in your new self-concept; revel in it every day if you can using the tools learnt in this book. Write down your goals and visualize them daily. It is possible that these simple steps take you on a trajectory you never thought was possible. When you see a blueprint, you suddenly see your dreams taking shape.

How badly do you want something? How strong is your desire to make it to the top? How fathomless is your inner urge? You've seen this drive, this urge in people that you believe are successful: there is something different about them, but you just don't know what it is. You can't seem to put your finger on it,

3   Daniel H. Pink, *Drive: The Surprising Truth About What Motivates Us,* Edinburgh: Canongate, 2009

but all you know is that the second they walk into a room –
there is something about the way they carry themselves – that
they must be someone important. You can see them embody
their drive.

You know that, if they don't already, they *will* get to where
they have to be.

The Bare Bones
LIFE LESSONS

From this chapter, you now know that

- To succeed, you need to desperately *want* to.

- The concept of volition implies that you can create your
  own destiny.

- Creating an inspiring self-concept is the starting point of
  success.

- Your self-concept can be anything you want it to be.

- Volition can be created, nurtured and developed.

- There are two kinds of people in this world: those
  motivated by intrinsic desires like passion, love and interest
  (Type I), and those motivated by extrinsic desires like
  money, fame and prestige (Type X). Type I invariably
  outperforms Type X.

What Do You Do Now?

10 **Change the Way You See Yourself.** Make a habit of bolstering your self-concept on a daily basis by chipping away at the negativity and replacing it with positive messages. Make self-belief a part of your self-talk and reacquaint yourself with your need to succeed on a daily basis. This will help shore up your own faith in yourself, and through that, your volition.

CHAPTER THIRTEEN

Wheel In, Walk Out

LESSONS LEARNT FROM POSITIVE THINKING

Depending on your situation, your career – or even your life – may sometimes resemble the plot for your very own film. You get a villain, a hero, a burning village and someone or something that needs to be saved. While this may sound suspiciously like a seventies movie, what remains the same is that a lot depends on the ending. The question then is – do you believe you have the power to write your own ending? And even if you did, what would that ending be?

How you see the ending pretty much defines you as an optimist or a pessimist. When life is going well, there is little difference between optimists and pessimists, but when things start to go bad, that is when the contrast becomes starker. Originally derived from the Latin word 'optimum', which means 'best', optimists are defined as those who view the final outcome as within their reach and expect the best results from a given situation or crisis. In 1985, Scheier and Carver further defined optimism as 'a generalized expectancy that good outcomes will generally occur when you confront problems across important life domains'.

Pessimists, not so much.

But why is this important? What is the payoff for looking at the bright side? Well, when you set out to change your work habits, you may find – as we have already discussed – that in the battle between new habits (masterminded by the frontal lobe) and old habits (spearheaded by the amygdala), the amygdala initially wins, pulling you back into the warm and loving embrace of comfort and familiarity, thus bringing you back to square one. For example, picking up a new skill or going back to your books mid-career or even taking a risk in your profession may initially lead you to feel that it is too hard and that you are rebelling against your natural 'instincts'. This feeling, or 'instinct', could be nothing but the amygdala talking, trying to set you back.

To counter this, you need to constantly motivate yourself to look at the brighter, bigger picture. This is where optimism comes in. We now know from previous chapters how the brain responds to the messages you give it; whether you give it a positive or negative message is entirely up to you. I cannot possibly understand what the payoff to pessimism is, but I can tell you that an outlook of negativity has greater chances of damaging a career, a marriage and a life.

Study after study has also shown that optimists are simply healthier. I find that to be true with my patients as well. I see a greater connection between patients who are positive about their surgeries and their outcomes. Very sceptical patients are usually those who are not happy with their results. If you have decided to go in for surgery, expect a good outcome, irrespective of the odds. Trust the surgeon and trust your decision. Moreover, there is also evidence that optimists are those who survive cancer longer than their more pessimistic counterparts.[1]

In *Flourish,* Martin Seligman has further outlined reasons for why optimists are better at beating disease:[2]

1. In general, optimists have chosen healthier lifestyles because they believe their actions matter. Pessimists, who are more fatalistic, believe that whatever they choose will not help. Optimists, quite simply, take better care.

2. Optimists have more friends and social support. The more love you have in your life, the lower the incidence of illness.

3. Optimists cope better with stress, which builds immunity.

---

1   Robert E. Franken, Human Motivation. 4th ed. VrPacific Grove, CA: Brooks/Cole Pub. Co.,1998

2   Martin E.P. Seligman, Flourish: *A New Understanding of Happiness and Well-being – and How to Achieve Them*, London: Nicholas Brealey Pub., 2011

In addition to this, when you see that something is achievable, it becomes that much more motivating for you to persevere, even if things don't always go your way. Seligman, also the author of *Learned Optimism,* believes that optimists see setbacks and failures as temporary and specific to a situation, and attribute them to factors that are external, not internal or within them, and they don't blame themselves as much. In other words, how you see the end result is integral to whether you persist or desist. You'll find that this is something which binds most successful people together: it is not that they *haven't* suffered soul-crushing defeats, but they have somehow managed to dust themselves off and pick themselves up.

On 17 December 1903, the Wright brothers succeeded in flying the first controlled, powered and sustained flight in their invention called the flyer, one of the earliest versions of what we now know as the modern airplane. But what many people don't know is that since other inventors were also trying to invent flying machines at the time, the local American press was less than impressed.[3] Undaunted, in 1908, the Wright brothers left for Europe with the intention of convincing the Europeans about the airplane and selling it to them. Their strategy worked. In Europe, they were treated like celebrities, hosted by royals and they began filling contracts for their planes before coming back to the United States in 1909. Thus making history.

Those who don't give up early on, as history has repeatedly shown us, go on to accomplish great things.

---

3   http://www.history.com/topics/inventions/wright-brothers; Last Access on 20 May 2016

Optimism is seen by many as a hard-coded trait that is so integral to a person's outlook that it is often used to define them. But can this be changed? Can it be taught? Well, as our brains are neither hardwired for optimism nor pessimism, the short answer is yes, it can be acquired, it can be learnt. Martin Seligman – along with Dr Steven Hollon of Vanderbilt University and Dr Arthur Freeman of the University of Medicine and Dentistry of New Jersey – developed the 'ABC-DE' technique of thinking which has its roots in the work of Albert Ellis, one of cognitive therapy's earlier leaders. The ABC-DE method is designed to ensure that people not only think positively, but also think more *accurately* when things don't go their way. Simply put, you can learn to be optimistic even if you aren't.

The best way I can explain the ABC-DE concept to you is to use a personal example. Fifteen years ago, I was a visiting consultant at a large corporate hospital in Mumbai. I would only perform endoscopic surgeries on women, which added up to a few sessions of operative work every week. Three years into working at this hospital, I was called in by the medical director I didn't think much of it, expecting to get a contract renewal letter. Instead, he apologetically handed to me a letter of discontinuation and said that while he liked me on a personal level, the board of directors had decided to terminate my contract based on the number of surgeries I had performed at the hospital. They were well within their rights to do so – in many hospitals, failure to perform a certain number of surgeries could lead to termination with no questions asked, no explanations given. I walked out with the letter in my hand, confused, disappointed and angry, all at the same time. Life had just handed me a lemon and I needed to figure out my next move.

The primary difference between optimists and pessimists is how they deal with adversity. According to the ABC-DE approach, the setback or adversity (A) leads us to interpret the setback in a particular way or belief (B), leading to the way we feel about it, which is the consequence (C). Using the paradigm of my case, my (A)dversity was that my operative and consultancy rights in the hospital were discontinued which led me to (B)elieve that I was not a good surgeon which (C) onsequently hampered my self-image. I had no idea what to tell either my colleagues or my patients. If you look at the way I handled this setback, it has all the hallmarks of a pessimist.

Now that we're done with the ABC, it's time to understand the D and E. Seligman says that there are two methods of dealing with negative or pessimistic thoughts: (D)istraction and (D)isputation. Distraction, depending on the situation, can be used to divert your attention from the problem at hand and do something else so as to not ponder and get further sucked into a negative-thought spiral. (D)isputation is to challenge your negative thoughts and argue with your *own* interpretations of the events that have unfolded. To (D)ispute effectively, you need to ask yourself the following four questions:

1. **What evidence do you have for your interpretation?**[4] In my case, all the letter said was that they wanted to terminate

---

4   Martin E.P. Seligman, *Flourish: A New Understanding of Happiness and Well-being – and How to Achieve Them*, London: Nicholas Brealey Pub., 2011

my services. There was no comment on my competence or my skills.

2. **What alternative interpretations are there?**[5] Let's assume my initial belief that I was a bad surgeon was untrue. What other reason could there be for the termination? Could it be that the medical director or board didn't like my specialty? Was it possible that someone more influential was threatened by my skills or popularity and didn't want me to continue work at the hospital?

3. **What are the implications for me if I take this position?**[6] If I persist with what I believed was the reason behind my termination, how would it affect me? In the larger scheme of things, how important was this adversity? Could I get visiting rights to other hospitals? Yes, I could. Could I take my patients to other hospitals? Yes, I could.

4. **How useful is my belief?**[7] If I persist with this belief, how will it help me in the future? Life doesn't always work out the way we'd like it to. So what could I have done differently?

To distract and dispute, it is important to be in tune with your feelings and correctly identify the ABCs of the situation. This method hinges on how well you can analyse your thoughts and the researchers who have developed this method indicate that by simply asking the right questions, we can get more deeply in touch with our inner dialogues.

---

5   Ibid
6   Ibid
7   Ibid

The final stage, (E)nergization, helps you take active steps to change your situation. In my case, I energized my situation by first trying to establish if what the management had said about the number of surgeries I had performed was, in fact, true. After taking a look at the OT register for the year – which detailed all the surgeries performed along with the date and the name of the surgeon – it turned out I was *not* the surgeon with the least number of surgeries. In fact, of the eight gynaecological surgeons, I was the third *highest*. I notified the medical director.

The next day I was reinstated.

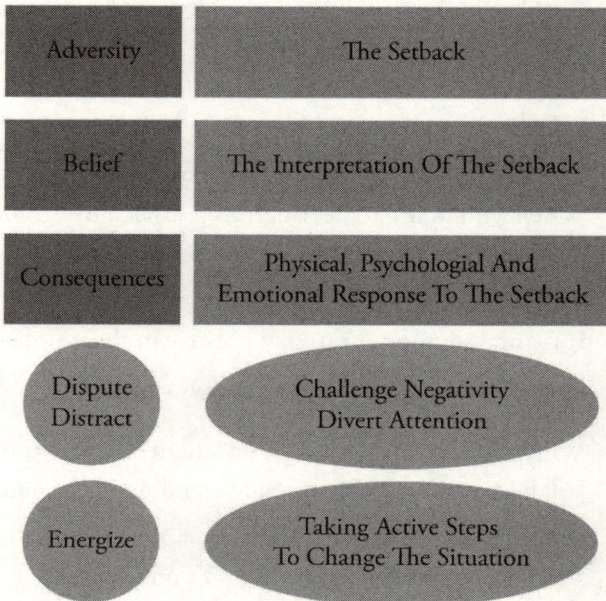

Adversity	The Setback
Belief	The Interpretation Of The Setback
Consequences	Physical, Psychologial And Emotional Response To The Setback
Dispute Distract	Challenge Negativity Divert Attention
Energize	Taking Active Steps To Change The Situation

Learn How to be Optimistic: The ABC-DE Method by Martin Seligman

When we see events as a catastrophe, we build up the worst-case scenario in our heads, which paralyses progress. Disputation as a process really helps to de-escalate the level of negativity and puts things into greater perspective. It enables us take steps borne from positivity not negativity. It is an important distinction. Using the ABC-DE method, our thinking patterns can change over time. We can learn to be optimists.

While there doesn't seem to be a payoff to pessimism because it is an essentially unproductive way of thinking, it is important to make the distinction between reckless and cautious optimism. In *Learned Optimism,* Martin Seligman goes on to establish that optimism shouldn't be used in every situation.[8] You should use optimism:

- When you want to achieve something like winning a match, getting promoted or making a sale.

- When you want to feel better – especially if you are depressed – or if you would like to boost your own morale.

- When you aren't feeling well and have to see a doctor. It is always important to stay positive in these situations.

However, being optimistic doesn't always work:

- When you're planning for an uncertain or risky future and you have no estimation or understanding of the outcome.

- When you're counselling others who seem to be in dire straits but whose context you don't understand.

---

8   Martin E.P. Seligman, *Learned Optimism: How to Change Your Mind and Your Life*, New York: Vintage Books, 2006

- When you decide to do things that you know are reckless at the outset, like drinking and driving.

If the cost of failure is very high, says Seligman – where your life or your entire career may be at stake – then optimism may not be the best choice for you.

Optimism must also be steeped in fact and not ignorance. A surgeon deciding whether a blood vessel will stop bleeding on its own, for example, is *not* correct in hoping for the best. That is when optimism is, quite simply, wishful thinking. It is crucial to know the difference.

Having said that, there are mainly benefits to thinking positive; you lose nothing by seeing the glass as half-full. Those who expect positive outcomes will always be more driven to succeed and are far more likely to get the ending they have always wanted.

The Bare Bones

Life Lessons

From this chapter, you now know that

- No one is born an optimist or a pessimist. Both are forms of *learnt* behaviour. You can learn to be an optimist.

- There is almost always a payoff to optimism; a negative outlook will never be as motivating as a positive one.

- There is a positive link between optimism and health.

- A positive outlook is what most successful people have in common – they are able to bounce back from disappointments far more easily.

- Those who don't give up early on, history has shown, go on to accomplish great things.

- There is a difference between cautious optimism and recklessness.

WHAT DO YOU DO NOW?

11 **Make Optimism Work for You.** Delay your reaction to adversity by waiting and then apply the ABC-DE exercise the next time you are faced with a challenge. Try to systematically and coolly analyse the reasons for your situation and find ways to change it.

CHAPTER FOURTEEN

Understanding Willpower
A SHORT NOTE

Like a set of New Year resolutions, you may write out a list of twenty things you wish to change about your working style. You may be motivated, inspired even, to renew your intentions and to make your career dreams come true. You may want to dust off that resume, sign up for skills training, have a heart-to-heart with your boss and bravely go where you haven't gone before. What I am about to tell you next completely contradicts any book on success and motivation. I can tell you that a few months in, there is a greater chance that the very list you've made will be used to line your drawer. That without strategizing and carefully planning the changes you want to make, you will be back to square one. Or maybe even ground zero because you'd feel worse than when you started off.

Willpower – used interchangeably with self-control for the purposes of this book – is a term that is most commonly associated with starting a good habit like eating healthy and exercising or kicking a bad habit like smoking or drinking. But whether you are aware of it or not, willpower is used by you every day in everyday decisions, from small ones to big ones, including the work habits you need to change to have a successful career. Willpower is not just that voice in your head telling you to stay away from that second cocktail. It is a physical process that entails the decisions you make *daily*, a process performed by your brain that expends energy and consumes glucose. It is like breathing, eating and sleeping.

For those of you who think that willpower is not your strong suit, you'd be surprised by how strong it already is. You use your willpower to not hit the snooze button on your alarm a third time and force yourself to wake up. You use your willpower to not snap at your spouse first thing in the morning simply because you're not a morning person. You use your willpower to leave half the dessert alone at dinner, laugh at the bad jokes your boss makes or not jump a red light in traffic.

Willpower is not a quality. It is not about whether you're a good or bad person. It is a reserve, a quota, a quantity of brain exertion. The more decisions we make that require self-control, the more we exhaust it and the more our reserves deplete. And once your reserves are empty, you're left vulnerable to bad decisions which sometimes have more serious consequences. It is disturbing to note, for example, how studies show that those on a diet are more likely to cheat on their spouse.[1]

---

1   Kelly McGonigal. *Maximum Willpower: How to Master the New Science of Self-Control*. London: Macmillan, 2012.

Thoughts

Emotions

What Drains Your Willpower

Peformance

Impulses

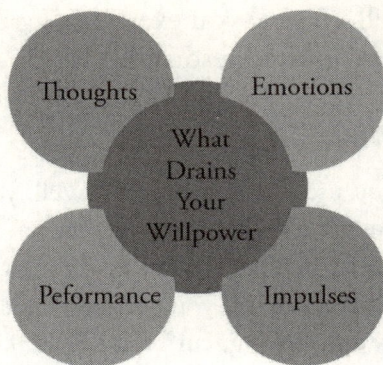

Willpower is usually the highest in the morning, but depletes through the day. And the tougher the decisions, the greater the struggle, the more the energy depleted and the lower the self-control. That is why it is harder to go to the gym at the end of a long work day or finish that article after dinner because you've used your willpower for so many things during the course of your day. Roy Baumeister and John Tierney, in their book *Willpower: Rediscovering the Greatest Human Strength*, have propounded the idea that 'self-control is like a muscle' – the more it is used, the more tired it gets. When not given adequate rest, this 'muscle' may completely break down, like extreme athletes who run themselves quite literally into the ground. But when not used, as Kelly McGonigal says in her book *Maximum Willpower*, 'Like a muscle, our willpower follows the rule of "use it or lose it". If we try to save energy by becoming willpower couch potatoes, we will lose the strength we have.' There are *two* things you must remember:

Willpower is a finite, limited resource.

All the self-control you exert during the day comes from this one limited resource.

Budgeting Willpower

So how do you use this information? Well, you can use it to budget your quota of willpower wisely. It can be best done by making strategic, intelligent choices through achieving your goals one goal at a time. If you decide that you would like to lose weight, stop smoking, cut back on drinking alcohol and meditate for an hour daily, *first* you must lose weight, *then* stop smoking, *then* cut back on drinking and so on. The harder the change, the more self-control you need to exert and the more draining the process. So in order to break habits you have had for decades, do them one at a time when it is not so stressful at work or at home. For example, if you're a man trying to lose weight when your wife has just delivered your first child, postpone that goal by a few months or more for when things have settled down.

THE MARSHMALLOW TEST

Walter Mischel's now iconic and seminal Marshmallow Test proved that the ability to delay gratification is essential for living a prosperous and satisfying life. Self-control not only predicts better academic performance, better social and cognitive functioning and better self-esteem, it also helps with stress management, achievement of goals and dealing with painful emotions.

The test involved a child being presented with a marshmallow and a choice. Either he or she could eat this one now, or wait and eat two later. From this, Mischel would attempt to understand the implications for the child's behaviour later in his life.[2]

Follow-up tests post-experiment established a greater connection between self-control and success. The children who waited to eat two marshmallows grew up to be teenagers who could resist temptation, had better concentration, were more intelligent, self-reliant and confident. When the same teenagers were adults in their twenties, they were more likely to have achieved their long-term goals, abstained from risky behaviour like substance abuse and were more educated, had better interpersonal skills and maintained their body weight far better than their counterparts with less self-control.

It has been proven that the ability to delay gratification is the key to success. It is believed that 'self-control is a better predictor of academic success than intelligence, a stronger determinant of effective leadership than charisma and more important for marital bliss than empathy.'[3]

2   Walter Mischel, *The Marshmallow Test: Understanding Self-Control and How to Master It*, London: Bantam Press, 2014

3   Kelly McGonigal, *The Willpower Instinct: How Self-Control Works, Why It Matters, and What You Can Do to Get More of It*, New York: Avery, 2013

Budgeting your self-control also means that you need to eliminate things or situations that unnecessarily drain you so that you can earn 'extra willpower points'. If you are a member of a local non-profit organization, a new parent, picking up a new skill at work and moonlighting as a home-making entrepreneur on the weekends, then you must eliminate something from your schedule to make room for a new goal. Or *identify your nuisance tumours*, (at the end of this chapter) like an unhealthy relationship with a colleague, unpaid bills or a small medical condition you've been ignoring for a while, and get them out of your life. The more unticked boxes you have or the more unnecessary situations you face, the more the stress will pile up, the harder the challenge will be and the more your self-control will deplete.

Boosting Willpower

Don't we all know someone who decided one sunny Tuesday in November that they would quit smoking? Fast forward to three years later and you find that they haven't touched a cigarette, they've stuck to their resolve and have never looked back. While all this time you've tried nicotine patches with little result. Why does self-control differ for different people? Why do some people make it look easy?

Scientists believe that there are three main reasons for this: one, *genes*. Genes play a significant role in determining just how much self-control you have. Some brains have stronger connections to the impulse or emotional centres of the brain, which is essential for a strong resolve. Some don't, leading to poor impulse control. Two, early childhood *learning* is surprisingly integral to willpower. If a child has been neglected or has felt unloved or abandoned, it could possibly interfere with the regular development of the brain. As part of a domino effect, these unfulfilled emotional needs impact a child's – and future adult's – ability to develop self-control because stronger, more primary emotions – like feeling threatened or harmed – have to be dealt with by the brain first, diverting its 'attention' from other functions. Three, *stress* can be a big roadblock to staying away from those cupcakes or declining the offer of something more serious like drugs. Emotional upheaval and stress interrupt the processing of impulse control and reduce your ability to say 'No'. Or 'Yes', as the case may be.

But despite what reserves you were born with or what environmental factors have led to its depletion, you can boost your willpower. One, physical exercise is believed by scientists to be like a 'wonder drug' to boost willpower. The scientific reason for this is that exercise stimulates the brain's prefrontal cortex which is where most of your self-control is exerted.

I Will, I Won't, I Want

Your brain has not one, but three parts that dictate self-control. Robert Sapolsky, a Stanford University neurobiologist, has propounded the idea that the primary function of the evolved prefrontal cortex is to 'make you do the harder thing'. It is that part of your brain which makes you opt for a low-calorie green tea when you want a sugary latte or makes you pull an all-nighter for that presentation when it is easier for you to just go to bed. The three parts of your brain that govern your self-control are the upper left side of the prefrontal cortex categorized as the 'I Will'[4] part which, for example, keeps you committed to long, tedious, stressful and mundane tasks even when all you want to do is give up and go home; the right region of the prefrontal cortex – referred to by scientists as 'I Won't' – is what controls your ability to resist cravings; finally, there is also an 'I want' component to your willpower, located in the lower and the middle of the prefrontal cortex, which keeps your long-term goals and needs in mind by ensuring that you stay true to what you want. But it is important to make a clear demarcation between the 'I Won't', the 'I Will' and the 'I Want' parts of your brains or else they won't work. Be clear. Your brain will deliver what you tell it to. The 'I will' and 'I won't' will only work if the brain understands the 'I want'. The question then is, what do you want?

Get as much exercise in, even if it is just for five minutes; anything that gets your heart rate up is good for you. Take care of your body. Two, sleep on time and get as much rest as your body needs. Even mild sleep deprivation over a significant period of time – like cutting an hour of sleep every night – could lead you to feel less in control, irritable, and less energetic, all of which

---

4   Kelly McGonigal, *The Willpower Instinct: How Self-Control Works, Why It Matters, and What You Can Do to Get More of It*, New York: Avery, 2013

could result in you feeling more stressed, more overworked and more prone to giving in to the impulse, for example, of telling your boss what you *really* think of him.

Three, eat your way into better self-control. Do note that whatever you eat – be it a piece of fruit or chocolate – gets converted into glucose. Your brain needs glucose, i.e., energy to make good decisions. Fuel your day through the food you eat so that you have stronger willpower. Having said that, do choose foods with slower release of sugars or foods that have a lower glycaemic index (GI) so that your body has a steady stream of glucose for a steady stream of good decisions. Sugary or high GI foods spike your blood sugar levels, but also send them crashing down, thus leaving you more vulnerable and open to bad decisions.

Four, rehearse your self-control. The more you practise saying 'No', the better you become at it. If this means walking out of a room when someone lights a cigarette when you're trying to quit, so be it. It will get easier to walk out of the room the next time, and then the next time. And soon, you will reach a point when you can sit in a room full of smokers without feeling the urge to light up.

Lastly, stress management is crucial to forging your self-control, and it is vital that you take active steps to mitigate stressful triggers. Do as many things that make you happy; whether it is meeting friends or catching up on your reading or spending time with your family. Happier people make better decisions.

It is not my opinion. It is, quite simply, science.

THE BIG FOUR
WHAT DRAINS YOUR WILLPOWER

While the most common association with willpower is trying to diet, willpower has more than just one meaning. Whether you know it or not, studies suggest that you exert self-control when you're trying to:

Control Your Thoughts – When you're trying to convince yourself that you are justified in taking a particular step or performing a particular action; for example, passing on confidential information to someone outside your firm. Only you have the ability to operate on this patient.

Control Your Emotions – When you're trying to pretend to be happy for a colleague when you've been passed up for a promotion or when you hold yourself back from unleashing your bad mood in a professional environment.

Control Your Impulses – This is the most common association with willpower, and this deals with your brain's ability to resist that extra cupcake after dinner or that urge to drink one more cocktail for the road.

Control Your Performance – This entails forcing yourself to focus on projects that need finishing despite being tired, lethargic or uninspired.

You use willpower for more things than you think. Any wonder then as to why making bigger changes is so hard?

IDENTIFY YOUR NUISANCE TUMOURS

Fibroids, one of the most common health conditions, usually occur in women in their reproductive years. One out of every four women across the world have fibroids. According to a study, about 14 million American women have been diagnosed with fibroids. The same study states that there are approximately 53.2 million women with fibroids in India.[5]

Even though various theories have been put forward, there is no known cause of fibroids. But what we do know is that even though most are benign and not dangerous, they can be a nuisance. They can cause lower abdominal pain, heavy menstrual bleeding and problems with fertility. They are 'nuisance tumours' and need to be removed.

I believe fibroids are a very apt metaphor for the numerous irritations, pending issues, small frustrations and unfinished businesses in our lives that drain our willpower. Jack Canfield, in his book The Success Principles, talks about these irritants and urges us to understand the 'cycle of completion'. So many of our projects are unfinished, and yet they stay on in our minds, taking up valuable space.

As we understood in 'Choosing to Choose', the human brain likes to complete loops and until a job is done

---

5   'Statistics by Country for Uterine Fibroids', http://www. rightdiagnosis.com/u/uterine_fibroids/stats-country.htm; Last Accessed on 17 August 2016

and the loop is closed, the brain still keeps the docket open. And the more the open dockets pile up, the more stressful and draining it is to do other things. Add to that the irritants we face on a daily basis and life becomes altogether overwhelming.

Perhaps it is the missing button on your favourite shirt that prevents you from wearing it to work, or a dripping tap that is keeping you up at night. Maybe it's the fact that your cell phone can receive texts but can't receive mails. There could be an unresolved fight that has been on your mind. You would be surprised at how the smallest unfinished things or the smallest issues can make a dent in your willpower and drain your brain because your energy is being diverted and divided. These brain drainers don't seem very threatening, but can be. Start to wrap up small projects in your life that look like this:

1. Cluttered drawers and cupboards
2. Stacks of documents and records that need sorting
3. Broken mirrors, stopped clocks, lifeless TV remotes and flickering tube lights
4. Unresolved fights
5. Unpaid bills
6. Broken household appliances
7. People that need your forgiveness
8. Collecting your clothes from the dry cleaners

You get the picture.

Trying to embark on the great project to change the course of your career will be that much harder when you're battling with the feeling of incompletion in other aspects of your life. Talane Miedaner, the author of Coach Yourself to Success, recommends consciously looking out for irritants by walking around your home or your office and taking note of all pending projects and unfinished businesses, and making a promise to yourself to get each one sorted out.[6]

The more you declutter your life, the more you declutter your brain. Therefore, the more self-control you have, the better your life will be.

The Bare Bones

LIFE LESSONS

From this chapter, you now know that

- Willpower or self-control is a limited resource.

- All the self-control you exert comes from this one finite resource.

- You need to budget your willpower to use it effectively — that is the reason why you shouldn't make too many big changes at once.

---

6   Talane Miedaner, *Coach Yourself to Success: 101 Tips from a Personal Coach for Reaching Your Goals at Work and in Life*, Lincolnwood, Ill.: Contemporary Books, 2000

- The amount of self-control you have depends – to a great extent – on:
  - Your genes
  - Early childhood learnings
  - Stress
- But willpower *can* be boosted. Use the following tools to enhance your self-control:
  - Exercise
  - Sleep
  - Proper nutrition
  - Practising willpower
  - Stress management

WHAT DO YOU DO NOW?

12 **Understand What Is Currently Draining Your Willpower.** If there are things you want to change in your life, identify them. It could be losing weight, getting a degree, taking a training course or quitting smoking. Next, understand the context of your life at the moment: is work very hectic? Are you expecting a baby? Are you moving cities? Understand where your life is in order to make a realistic attempt to achieve your goals. Lastly, list the little things that may interfere with your ability to accomplish these goals by identifying your nuisance tumours. Change is just around the corner.

CHAPTER FIFTEEN

Primum Non Nocere
FIRST, DO NO HARM

It is the first thing they teach you in medical school. It is the backbone of any good, ethical medical practice. Whatever be the procedure, surgery or medical advice being dispensed, at the core *must* lie the interests and well-being of the patient. Primum Non Nocere. First, do no harm. But it doesn't stop harm from being done. It doesn't stop unethical medical practices from being followed. It doesn't stop doctors from ordering a battery of tests that patients don't need. Or pharmaceutical companies pushing expensive drugs when cheaper generics are available. It also doesn't stop, in extreme cases, the forcing of life-altering procedures like hysterectomies on perfectly healthy women in their twenties and thirties.

Like in any other profession, harm is being done by doctors with premeditation, malicious intent, complete awareness and with full realization of the consequences of their actions. But sometimes, also like in other professions, doctors with the best of intentions and the deepest of consciences inadvertently harm – as we have seen in the pages of this book – and spend their lives living with things they wish they could change. This, the brief endnote of *The Anatomy of Success,* will leave you with what is core to good medical practice, how it applies to you and just a few thoughts on how you can avoid doing harm to both your career and yourself. Even though it is the last thing I leave you with, I hope it is the *first* principle you apply when you are trying to choose – as Viktor Frankl puts it – 'meaning for yourself'.

First, do no harm to yourself. When finding meaning in both your life and career, find something that makes you happy, employs the best of your talents, and makes you get up and look forward to the everyday. Resist working with people you don't like, in companies that have a dubious approach to ethics and in work cultures that don't encourage free thought. Resist working just for the superficialities of money, prestige and perceptions of upward mobility since they will ultimately lose their charm. Don't put work before yourself, your health and your needs. Don't let clients dictate your holidays, your sleep cycle and your meal times. As a doctor, I can tell you this: stress *will* find a way to infiltrate your immunity.

Second, do no harm to your family. Kids grow up, parents become old and marriages may fray. And all of this as you spent the best years of your life in stuffy boardrooms and tiny cubicles. Even though you might feel you are doing this for your family, try to focus on both the journey *and* the destination. Even if you are doing this for your future, please know that the seeds of the very future you are working so hard towards are being sown in the present. There is a richness to a well-rounded life that cannot be bought, cannot be substituted and cannot be counterfeited.

Third, do no harm to your profession. Let your profession grow, be a credit to it. Work according to the standard you set for yourself. Create environments that are positive, transparent, efficient and excellent. Don't compete against anyone but yourself. Looking over your shoulder distracts you from looking straight ahead. There may also come a time when you are forced to choose between what you need to do and the *right* thing to do. Weigh such decisions carefully and try to do as little harm as possible.

Success at just about any cost will leave you poorer in the end, no matter what.

You can have all the money in the world, but it is meaningless without someone to share it with. You can ascend to the CEO throne, but it is pointless if you are diagnosed with health problems. You can have all the love in the world, but if you can't provide for your children, it will affect your relationships in one way or another. The art of maintaining a fine balance is also the hardest lesson I have ever had to learn and it is one that I keep learning every day of my life.

Two Harvard professors, Laura Nash and Howard Stevenson, provided a more multi-dimensional view of professional success in their book *Just Enough: Tools for Creating Success in Your Work and Life.* In it, they expanded on the fact that even people whom society would regard as successful are looking for 'something more'.[1] Money, prestige and professional heights were not seen as enough. Nash and Stevenson elaborated on Jim Warner's study of 200 CEOs culled from the stellar Young Presidents Organization. The CEOs who were interviewed felt they were missing out on something which the researchers call the 'Success Versus' view. High professional achievers felt whatever they had achieved was at the cost of something else: 'Success versus family, success versus self, success versus society'.[2] Nash and Stevenson further identified four categories for success to have any meaning: the first is **happiness**, which has been defined in terms of contentment with your life and a feeling of pleasure. The second, **achievement**, are goals accomplished that are regarded as favourable by others and the self. The third, **significance,** is defined as a positive impact on loved ones and the fourth, **legacy,** is defined as instituting values or accomplishments in such a way that others will find future success.

But can work alone provide these four satisfactions? According to me, these parameters of success as defined by Nash and Stevenson are sound, yes, but can only have meaning if they resonate over the four main areas that govern our overall well-being. If I could bottle it up into a formula and lay it all out, I would put those areas into four quadrants, four sections, four parts:[3]

---

1   Laura L. Nash, and H. Howard Stevenson, *Just Enough: Tools for Creating Success in Your Work and Life*, Hoboken, N.J.: John Wiley & Sons, 2004

2   Ibid

3   Ibid

Personal	Professional
Spiritual	Family

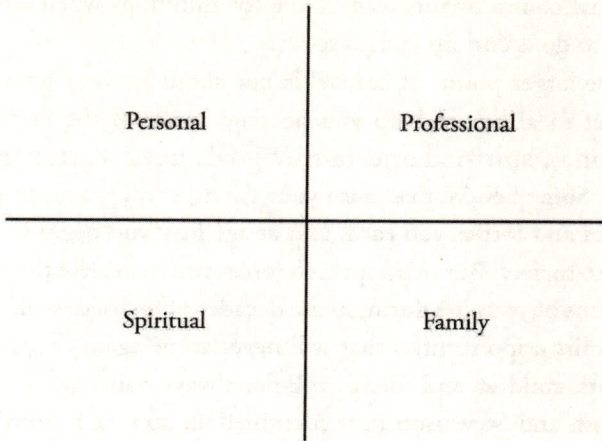

The Perfect Balance

To me, it is important to attain the four satisfactions of achievement, happiness, legacy and significance in *each* of the areas above: personal, spiritual, professional and family. That is when, to me, true success will be achieved.

Professional achievement requires long nights, time away from your children, and time stolen from yourself, draining you of the energy or the inclination to find your spiritual self – how is it possible when there are unpaid bills, unresolved fights or constant worries about your family? It is hard when you have to force yourself not to answer work calls when you're on vacation. It is hard when work means you have to miss your child's school plays. It is difficult for new mothers to balance their ambitions with childcare. Sometimes maintaining your life's basic equilibrium seems like work, marriages seem like work, household responsibilities seem like unpaid labour and spiritual commitments seem like lofty ambitions when all you want to do is curl up and go to sleep.

The larger point, of course, is not about striving for some perfect ideal but to help you become aware of the fact that personal, spiritual and family goals need a strategy as well. Some believe that until your twenties you learn, in your thirties and forties you earn, and at age fifty you begin to give back to society. But this approach forces you to neglect the other domains of your life during these decades of focused work. You may miss opportunities that will never come again as spouses, parents, children and friends will not always wait.

Nash and Stevenson have identified an approach called the 'Spiralling and Linking Strategy' where a person can move between their various goals on a daily, and sometimes minute-by-minute, basis in each of the domains of their life previous[4]. For example, waking up early to meditate and exercise followed by putting in a full day at work, then followed by coming home on time and spending quality hours with the family ensures that all four quadrants of spiritual, personal, family and professional goals are met in one day.

To pull this off, you need motivation, discipline and conviction that what you are striving for is worth the fight. Maybe your four quadrants will be different from mine, but the important thing to remember is that it is ultimately about the legacy you leave behind. No matter what choice you make, it is all about reaching the end of your life knowing that you had the fullest, richest and the most glorious experience of it.

---

4   Ibid

The Anatomy of My Success
ACKNOWLEDGEMENTS

I truly wouldn't have been where I am today if it were not for the hundreds of people who have been there to love, guide, teach, support, motivate and inspire me during the incredible journey I have been on. I'd like to extend a big thank you to:

To my parents, Swaran and Yagyavir Sinha, for their inspiration. Thank you for teaching me the value of hard work.

To Dr Manju Sinha, my wife and anaesthesiologist. I wouldn't have achieved anything if it wasn't for your love and dedication.

To Rinkita, Pawan, Rushindra and Gautami, my children. You mean the world to me.

To Gayatri Pahlajani. If it wasn't for you, this book would not have been possible. You have helped me become an author. Thank you very much.

To Rachna and Gopal. Thank you for guiding me.

To Ratna and Himender. Thank you for all your support during my formative years.

To Mr and Mrs Arora, my in-laws, for being so loving.

To Vandana and Devinder Arora, Kanchan and Pinto for being there.

To Shalu, Indu, Anita and Milind for becoming family.

To Neeta Warty for being such a great friend.

To D. Sivanandhan, my dear friend. Thank you for having the confidence and faith in me to train senior police and CBI officers.

To Jack Canfield and Patty Aubery for all their help during the Train the Trainer Program in 2012. Thank you, Jack, for agreeing to be a part of this book.

To Naazia, thank you for your untiring effort in putting this manuscript together.

To Dr Gayatri Rao and Dr Shweta Raje. Thank you for your immeasurable help and for looking after the patients at the times I was writing this book.

To Dr Meenakshi, Dr Aparna and Dr Chaitali for all the scientific papers and workshops.

To Mr Siddique and Ms Shirin for setting me on the path to achievement. You laid the foundation and for that, I thank you.

To Sangeeta and Snehal. Thank you for taking care of my financial health. And thanks to the late Dinesh Shah.

To Aruna and Inder Mookhey for all your help.

To Dr Shirish Sheth. Thank you for your help for my training in London.

To Brij Mehra, thanks for being a great friend.

To Geeta Rao for all your support.

To Dr Tehemton Udwadia and Dr Gadgil. Thank you for trusting me at CeMAST, and for allowing me to use its images. And thanks to you, Purnima and Pradip Raheja.

To Dr Sanjay Oak. Thank you for inspiring me to write.

To Dr Parveen Bhatia and Dr Sunil Jindal. Thank you for being such great friends.

To Rajesh Jain and Timmy Kandhari for being great business advisors.

To Jitendra Grover, Vaidheesh and Asawari at EISE.

To my friends Mahesh, Rita, Deepak Desai, Vikram, Ravi, Pravin and Abhijit, Deepak and Neeta Rajani, O.P. Sharma and Vinod Chandiramani for being there for me.

To my teachers Adam Magos, Harry Reich, CY Liu, James Danielle, Kurt Semm, Bernard Chern and Dr C.M. Alwani.

To late professor Shivdasani for inspiring me and to late Mr Nazareth for the help in training me in the art of public speaking.

To Adlakhas at Amritsar and Vinod Vohra at Indore for their belief in me.

To Karthika V.K., editor-in-chief at HarperCollins India, for seeing the potential of this book, and to Debasri Rakshit and Rea Mukherjee, editors at HarperCollins India, in shaping that potential.

To Mr Rangan and Mr Vasant for helping me set up my hospital.

To Deepak Parekh, Kirthiga Reddy, Vinay Hebbar, Jagdeep Kapoor, Dr Radhakrishnan Pillai, Harish Nadkarni, Nandan Savnal, Ninad Tipnis, and Praveen Kalawar for the advance praise.

To Divarkar Rana, Amit Sharma and Ashwini Kumar for your help in my journey into endoscopy.

To Devang Mehta for introducing me to 3D laparoscopy.

To Gurmukh Advani.

To all the staff at Women's Hospital, Dr Rishita, Dr Arundhati, Dr Namrata, Dr Kaushal, Mary, Arti, Dharmishta, Sangeeta, Leena, Sucheta and just about everybody who makes it worthwhile coming in to work.

I would also like to express my gratitude to all my students; who actually taught me more than they know.

And finally, to all my patients. Thank you for placing your trust in me.

I hope I can continue to do justice to all those who have helped me along the way and to those I can help in the future.